D1577929

Praise for The Yes Book

"What a rich read! […]You would be a fool to say No to this book. Where else can you find such a rich trove for your life's illumination by the affirmative?"

—**Kim Stafford**
author of *The Muses Among Us: Eloquent Listening and Other Pleasures of the Writer's Craft*

"Look, there are old bloody murderous greedy stupid criminal stories, like those so beloved of Bin Laden and Stalin and Hitler and Mao and Pol Pot, and then there are far bigger better wilder more piercing stories, stories that might finally put those other older stories out of business someday. These bigger stories are of hope and grace and defiant courage against darkness and fear and murder and terror and smoke and fire and ash. They are the stories of what people are capable of far beyond the old stories of blood. Here's one of these bigger better stories."

—**Brian Doyle**
award-winning author of *Mink River*,
on his *Yes Book* story "Dawn and Mary"

"[*The Yes Book*] is a powerful compendium of yeses, a litany of yeses, a choir that praises the one word we long to hear and love the best. Yes."

—**Dorianne Laux**
author of *Facts about the Moon*

"I love the premise of this book—the idea of exploring all the creative and thought-provoking ideas about such a simple concept as what is meant by 'yes!' It was delightful to experience the varied, rich, creative expressions in this collection and I recommend exploring it to anyone who wants to better understand what embracing 'yes' truly means."

—**Mira Kelly**
author of *Beyond Past Lives*

"*The Yes Book* is a wonderful collection of prose and poetry inspiring the reader to say Yes to Life trusting that when the Time is Ripe, Yes will bear the sweetest fruits of all."

—**Deborah Maragopoulos**
FNP, author of *LoveDance: Awakening the Divine Daughter*

"What a wonderful project! I have never had my mind, heart and soul juggled at the hands of words like I have with *The Yes Book*.

—**Rome Esmaili**
artist, world traveler

"The power of saying yes is such an urgent and timely message for both men and women all over the world, and I know this book will at once soothe and empower many hungry souls."

—**Linda Thompson Whidby**
writer

"Brilliant!"

—**Lisa Hoffman-Reyes**
author

"The Exult Road website, and *Yes Book* are beautiful. Congratulations on accomplishing important work in such an appealing package. "

—**Maureen Buchanan Jones, Ph.D.**
author of *Maud & Addie*

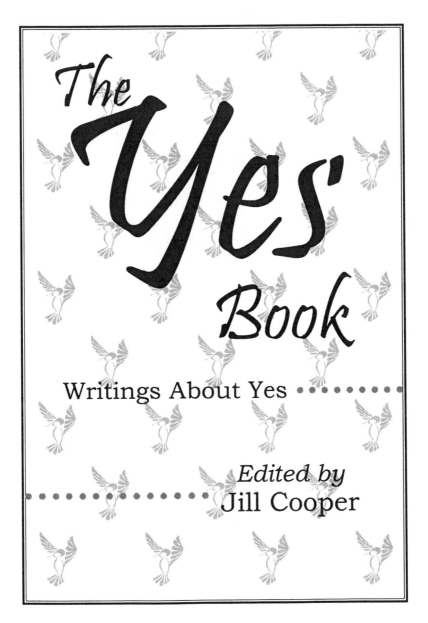

The Yes Book

Writings About Yes · · · · · · · · · ·

· · · · · · · · · · · · · · · *Edited by*
Jill Cooper

EXULT ROAD

EXULT ROAD

Published by Exult Road
Copyright © 2014 by Exult Road.
All rights reserved.

No part of this book may be reproduced, stored in a retrieval system, or transmitted in any form, by any means, including mechanical, electronic, photocopying, recording, or otherwise, without prior written permission of the publisher.

Exult Road
Email: publisher@exultroad.com

Certain of these writings have previously appeared in print and are here reprinted with permission: "Unschackled" and "Silent Seat" by Tosha Silver published in Make Me Your Own; poems to the divine beloved. Copyright © 2013. Reprinted by permission. "Inception" by Joanne S. Bodin published in Adobe Walls #5, An Anthology of New Mexico Poets. Reprinted by permission. "For Writers," by Maureen Buchanan Jones. Reprinted by permission. Joseph Millar: "Dark Harvest" from Overtime, published by Eastern Washington University Press. Copyright © 2001 by Joseph Millar. Reprinted by permission. "Let's" by Ellen Bass, from Like a Beggar. © BOA Editions, Ltd., 2002. Reprinted by permission. "The Thing Is" by Ellen Bass. Mules of Love. Port Townsend, Washington: Copper Canyon Press, 2014. Reprinted by permission. "Dawn and Mary" by Brian Doyle. Reprinted by permission.

ISBN 978–0-9905317–0-8 (softcover)
978–0-9905317–2-2 (ebook)

Printed in the United States of America

For Jon

Contents

yes is a world
& in this world of yes live
(skillfully curled)
all worlds
—e.e. cummings

Foreword

Dorianne Laux

I once sat under the stars in a hot tub in Marin County with a gaggle of women, each with her own specific musical pitch of laughter, each with her own particular pain. One of us told a story about a friend who'd suffered a stroke and was stricken with Broca's aphasia which, in its most severe form, reduces spoken utterance to a single word. For the first time that evening, silence descended. We sipped at our ice water; or we sat on our hands and let our thighs float to the surface, watching them bob below us like distant islands; or we turned over like seals and offered our backs or our bellies to the air, our warmed flesh tightening as it cooled.

We could hear the lost freeway below us swimming with cars and the occasional harrumph of a semi truck or moving vans packed with precious cargo, then a vicious but short-lived cat fight, a high-pitched scream, then nothing, and the night pulled its black cloak back over its shoulders. In the quiet, each of us must have pondered what the world might be like without language, without this sense of community and communion we had all wrested from our busy calendars, looking up at—and then away from—the faces before us. Someone finally asked: "If you were left with only one word, what would it be?"

We went around the circle, each woman saying a word. Laughter again, snorts and howls, the water splashing under our hands. I don't remember most of the words that were offered that night, not even my own. And yet I probably remember that night only because of the one word I do recall. The friend who had brought me was a poet, translator, essayist, and editor, also a Buddhist, a cook, a horsewoman, and an orchard worker. She moved with grace and had an accurate and acute mind, one that turned a question over like a peach, looking for the bruise just under the skin, or lifted the shod hoof of a horse with a tenderness that was almost as painful to watch as the pebble sluiced from the cleft with the blunt edge of a butter knife.

When it was her turn to answer, she said, "Yes." One woman tilted her head, as if the word was preface to the word she was going to say, and then someone else got it and laughed, and then we all laughed and struck up a spontaneous conversation using only the word *yes*. "Yes," nodding in delight, "yes, yes," said twice in excitement, a sonorous "yes," a hesitant "yes," a whispered, hurried, or resounding "yes." The lecherous, reverent, hilarious "yes," the piteous "yes," the "yes" that accepts pain and suffering, the "yes" of forgiveness and regret. That is the word I have remembered from that night, the word that this book meditates on in stories and poems, a powerful compendium of yeses, a litany of yeses, a choir that praises the one word we long to hear and love the best. Yes.

Dorianne Laux
Raleigh, North Carolina
2014

Introduction

This book was created through a chorus of yeses.

I was originally inspired to publish *The Yes Book* by the mantra, "Say yes to everything you can as soon as you can," by author and teacher Lola Jones. Uplifted by the idea of Yes, and how good it felt to repeat the word, I wrote a poem celebrating and affirming all sorts of daily events and emotions. I felt a deep exhale, a sense of relief, and excitement in the possibilities of Yes.

Posted on the Internet, the poem touched a number of people, and blogger/writing teacher Heather Rader was moved to "answer" the poem with her own Yes piece. She also used the original poem in her class as a seed for an exercise encouraging the students to create their own Yes works. They responded with a diverse array of inspiring writings, expanding the momentum of Yes. The idea to gather writings on the word *Yes* for a book and website collection was born.

The Yes Book call for submissions created a stir. We asked: *What do you embrace? What does Yes mean to you, your family, the world? How has saying Yes transformed your life?* Stories, essays, and poetry poured in from a wide variety of voices—from well-established, best-selling authors to bright new stars. Women and men of all ages from around the world shared their stories of Yes.

Writers opened up their creative veins and spilled gold into words. Some told stories of shining hope, heroism, recovery, peace, and joy. Others shared the sacred power of saying Yes to being their truest selves. Others explained the subtle Yes in such personal and surprising ways; the world is better for the telling.

From their words you will learn the science of Yes on the brain. You will feel the pulse of Yes in the heart. You will know the bliss of Yes as a practice in daily life. You will witness the shadows of Yes and peer into the mysterious worlds that open with the key of Yes.

The Yes Book makes the world brighter, and we hope you use the power of Yes to invite more good into your own lives. We also hope you share *The Yes Book* with everyone. The book itself is a transformational device. Yes is catching. Spread the wonder.

On behalf of all the editors, with deepest gratitude and love,

Jill Cooper
Editor
Underwood, WA
2014

Part One

Yes

Word

Fred LaMotte

Now I begin my opus.
All my life I've prepared for this.
I see it now, a poem of one Word.
A wild insouciant light-bearing Word
that thrills the heart of a gnat
and spins ten million suns
from the black hole of silence
on the tip of the tongue—
a Word that oscillates each atom
and quickens the amygdala with hope
in the reptilian brain
of the angry politician—
a Word so hot it shocks
that veiled lady Night
into revealing the starry algorithms
of her dance, and at dawn
her lavender fingers stroking the mist away—
oh my one sweet single-syllabled
gong of impeccable magic,
charged with the super-conductive
quantum uncertainty
of poetic justice,
so quietly and elegantly
transforming the cosmos
into a drop of honey...
Someone has spoken it!
Praise the murmurer...yes.

Say Yes: Balboa Academy 2014 Graduation Speech

Silvio Sirias

I floundered for several weeks, searching for something meaningful to share with you on this special day. But the harder I tried, the more elusive my quest became. Although I seldom suffer from writer's block, I was now adrift in a sea of useless ideas, crossing out page after page of false starts.

When I thought about my difficulties, I traced them back to when you were ninth-graders and, for reasons that still remain a mystery to me, the Class of 2014 earned a special place in my heart. Because of this, when you invited me to be your commencement speaker, the honor soon became a millstone around my neck, and the weight of delivering a message of consequence grew heavier each passing day.

I was on the verge of panicking when, unexpectedly, inspiration struck. The muse greeted me the instant my wife and I stepped into the home of a fellow teacher. There, stenciled on the living room wall in large, attractive letters was the phrase:

You are living your story.

I let out a long sigh of relief because I knew that, at last, the drought had ended. There, calling out to me, was the idea I wish to share with you today.

You are living your story.

As I have often told you, we have the power to make our stories wondrous—full of love, light, hope, and beauty. This is one of the main reasons you've been going to school all these years, and certainly one of the reasons you're going off to college—the more educated you become, the more control you'll have over your narratives. There is nothing in life more empowering, I assure you, than the ability to chart the course of our stories.

When I reminisce about you as ninth-graders, I think about how malleable you were back then. Eager to please your new teachers, you were easy to bend, mold, and shape. Your eyes glowed with excitement every day. Your hearts brimmed with high expectations of everyone and everything: your schoolmates, your teachers, and the world. Yes, beyond a doubt, as ninth-graders you were naïve and easy to fool.

Over the last four years, however, a small measure of cynicism has trickled into your lives. By that I mean that you now mistrust the values your elders have been trying to teach you. But we need not be concerned over this. It is only natural. It happens to everyone on the road to adulthood. I say that we don't need to be concerned because I have witnessed that you and your Balboa Academy schoolmates have an optimistic outlook. I've seen your selflessness in the houses you've built for others, the people you've clothed and fed in times of need, the countless smiles you've placed on the faces of the less fortunate, and the work you've done to slow down the clock of ecological doom. Wherever you go from here, then, please endeavor to keep cynicism at bay, and please, continue your efforts to make the world a better place.

As your Spanish teacher, instead of making you jump through grammar hoops, by way of poems and stories I tried to fill your hearts with the beauty of language. I also wanted to make these great achievements of the human imagination an essential part of your lives. I wanted you to understand that a poem, a story, or a novel can serve as a beacon during those times when we've lost our sense of direction, because, I now warn you, your life, like everyone else's, will contain painful events. As César Vallejo wrote in *Los heraldos negros*: "*Hay golpes en la vida, tan fuertes . . . ¡Yo no sé!*'" ("There are in life such hard blows . . . I don't know!") Sentiments such as the one the Peruvian poet expressed with sparking clarity can put things into perspective and help us get our lives back on track when our stories have been momentarily derailed. Great tales, when closely examined, reveal our potential, our strengths, and even our claims to sainthood.

Remember, then, that it is important to study the stories of others as you live your own. You have often heard me speak with reverence of the Aristotelian concept of *imitatio*. In this construct, the Greek philosopher advises artists who aspire to greatness to imitate the best models. That's the starting point. The outstanding painters, sculptors, architects, musicians, and writers of the Renaissance took Aristotle's message to heart, raising the level of human expression to the loftiest heights in Western civilization.

What Aristotle suggested for artists over two millennia ago works well for writing our own life stories. To succeed, all you need is the commitment and the discipline to follow these five steps: pick a worthy model, study your model intently, learn the vocabulary necessary to understand and discuss your model, and then write your story following the example. Ah, but then comes the hard part: you need to keep revising until your story surpasses the quality of the original.

If you follow Aristotle's teachings conscientiously, imitating excellent models as you live your own story, you can achieve anything.

Imitatio.

To demonstrate that I practice what I preach, before committing these thoughts to paper I consulted a few outstanding models of commencement speeches. For me to presume to offer better advice that what these contain would be absurd. And since I wholeheartedly agree with the wisdom they impart, I will take the liberty to capsulize them for you.

President John F. Kennedy pleaded with the Harvard Class of 1963 to believe in and to work for world peace. "No problem of human destiny is beyond human beings," he stated on that occasion.

More recently, the novelist Barbara Kingsolver, speaking at Duke University, told the Class of 2008 to reject the emphasis that modern society places on accumulating wealth. In doing so, she said, we commit to using less resources and the healing of the planet will begin.

The Pulitzer Prize–winning journalist Russell Baker advised the 1995 Class of Connecticut College to take the time to listen to the life that surrounds us, as well as to what's in our hearts.

In addressing Syracuse University's Class of 2013, the writer George Saunders stressed the importance of being kind. In his speech, he asked, "Who, in your life, do you remember most fondly, with the most undeniable feelings of warmth? Those who were kindest to you, I bet."

Getting closer to the crux of today's message, Steven Jobs urged Stanford's Class of 2005 to have the courage to follow their hearts and their intuition. "Stay foolish, and stay hungry," he counseled.

I was delighted to discover that the idea that we live our stories was at the heart of several of my models.

Conan O'Brien told Harvard's Class of 2000 not to fear making mistakes. He said, "Fall down, make a mess, break something occasionally. And remember, whatever happens, the story is never over."

The actor Bradley Whitford, who played the role of the president's adviser in the television series *The West Wing*, urged the Class of 2006 of The University of Wisconsin to take action. Only in taking action, he noted, can we become the heroes of our own stories.

And I'll conclude with the model that most closely resembles the spirit of what I've tried to share with you today. Speaking at Knox College to the Class of 2006, Stephen Colbert told the graduates to avoid cynicism. He highlighted the need to trust others, as well as the need to believe in ourselves and in our communities. "Cynicism," he said, "is a self-imposed blindness, a rejection of the world because we are afraid it will hurt us or be disappointed in us. Cynics always say no ... for as long as you have the strength to, say yes."

And so, in parting, I ask Balboa Academy's Class of 2014 to always say yes to finding and imitating exceptional models, to say yes to working for world peace, to say yes to living in simplicity, to say yes to taking the time to listen, to say yes to committing acts of kindness, to say yes to staying foolish and hungry, to understand that it's okay to occasionally make a mess of things, to say yes to taking action, and, more importantly, to go forth and make your life a story that inspires others.

Yes

Jill Cooper

Yes to this day.
Yes to your body.
Yes to what your true body
wants.
Yes, to the insides
of flowers.
Yes to opera. Yes to trees.
Yes to being late.
Yes to driving
the kids back and
forth back and
forth and back.
Yes to home.
Yes to your lover.
Yes to being
alone.
Yes to your dreams.
Yes to your best stories.
Yes to feeling
everything you feel.
Yes to feeling
anything you feel.
Yes, yes, yes.
Yes to avocado skins
in the sun on
the counter of your
best ideas. Yes

to vacations with
people you like.
Yes to the talking person
on the plane.
Yes to the crying babies.
Yes to your best work.
Yes to your effortless
work. Yes to free time.
Yes to tea and chocolate.
Yes to waiting. Yes
to finding out the
truth. Yes to trying and
not trying. Yes to saying
no. Yes to beets. Yes
to soft towels and knowing
how to say yes to your life.
Yes to conscious love
on our planet.
Yes to peace, yes
to what is. Yes to yes.
Yes to Browning and
Keats. Yes to Sandburg
and Oliver. Yes to Dylan
and strum. Yes to storm
and sun. Yes to yes. Yes
to soup, and to sleeping,
and to eternal yeses.
Yes to permission and
to magnets, to bells, and
magnificence. Yes to your
smile, to your slowness,
to your waiting. Yes
to your impatience to your
glory to your determination
Yes to your effortlessness.
Yes
to the velvet underneath
your tongue. Yes to your

smile to your chin to your
eyes. Yes to your creations.
Yes to your go. Yes to your
stop. Yes to the class, the
kitchen, the lab, the beach,
the greenhouse, the concrete
city, the sea. Yes to resilience,
and yes to going toward.
Yes to dropping resistance,
yes to softening. Yes to yes.
Yes to that dance creeping
up your spine. Yes to
presents, the snow plough,
the car, the soap, the paint.
Yes to the dogwood,
the rose, the cat. Yes to
feeling good, yes to crying
sometimes, yes to today.
Yes to now. Yes to you.

Your Brain on "Yes"

Andrew B. Newberg, M.D.

Yes is one of the most interesting words, neurobiologically speaking. Studies show that the word *yes*, as well as other positive words, activates a variety of areas in the brain that support our positive emotions and our reward system, including the orbitofrontal cortex, basal ganglia, and limbic system. *Yes* makes us feel good, gives us optimism, and enables us to perform more effectively. How does it accomplish all this?

To a large extent, *yes* provides substantial meaning for us because of how we are raised. We always hear the word *yes* when we do something good, avoid something bad, or make someone feel better. Think about the times you heard the word *yes* growing up. Maybe it was for a good report card, when you took out the trash without being asked, or when you were helping an elderly person cross the street.

We know from brain studies that both animals and humans who receive positive affirmations over a period of time end up having more connections in their brain. They are more creative and seek out novelty more effectively. "Yes" does us good!

As with all words, a substantial component of the word *yes* is also the emotions and actions that accompany it. So when you heard the word *yes*, you saw smiles, you received hugs, and you were encouraged to repeat the rewarded action. These other elements that accompany the word are extremely important. Studies suggest that as much as 80 percent of what is communicated occurs through facial expressions and body language. Words themselves are only a small part of our communications.

The changes that occur in the brain in response to the word *yes* most likely result from a variety of different neurotransmitters (such as acetylcholine, glutamate, and dopamine) that not only make us feel good inside but actually stimulate the growth of other neurons. That is why when we hear the word *yes* and experience the positive emotions behind it, our brain actually begins to grow as individual nerve cells reach out and create new connections. This is the brain biologically saying *yes*, growing neuronal connections that allow more brain activity to occur in the future.

The brain itself is built to a large extent upon the "yes" and "no" dichotomy. "Yes" neurons, also called excitatory, become more active and stimulate other neurons to become more active. "No" neurons are inhibitory and block activity in other areas of the brain. So our brain is always in a balance between yes and no. The more we hear the word *yes*, the more the "yes" or excitatory neurons begin to fire, increasing the connections and the interactions between different nerve cells. This process can sometimes be described by the concept that "neurons that fire together wire together." Since neurons that fire together augment their connections, we become interested in repeating whatever action brought on the word *yes*.

Of course, the opposite is also true. When we hear the word no, that activates our stress system in the brain, which includes our amygdala, insula, and hypothalamus. These structures activate whenever anything bad happens to us and cause a release of neurotransmitters and hormones that make us feel bad. It's interesting to note that repetitive stimulation of these negative pathways, along with the stress response, actually results in a less well functioning brain. Animal studies have shown that the brains of animals who are raised in nonsupportive, highly stressful environments have very few connections between nerve cells. Likewise, their behavior is that of animals who are scared, uncertain of the world, and lacking in creativity and novelty seeking. In human beings, excessive exposure to negative words such as no results in increased reactivity to stress, increased anxiety and depression, and a poorer sense of well-being.

A corollary of the word *yes* may be a sense of optimism. Optimism itself has been shown to have substantial benefits to our overall health and wellness. In fact, long-term health studies have shown that those individuals who express the highest levels of optimism tend to have far fewer problems with heart disease, cancer, and other illnesses. Optimistic people live longer than those who are less optimistic.

Yes is a powerful word. *Yes* can support positive behaviors, encourage creativity, and improve our overall health and well-being. Focusing on the word *yes* and other affirmations provides great advantage whether preparing for school, a job, an athletic event, or a date. The release of dopamine and other good neurotransmitters associated with the word *yes* helps you interact more successfully with other people, allows you to respond better in stressful situations, and leads you to a higher quality of life.

In my own life, the word *yes* has been an essential element that has enabled me to pursue many lifelong goals. I have sought out possibilities and explored and followed my passions in a positive way. By focusing on what can be done rather than what can't, I have found that I can be more creative and solve problems more effectively. My friends, family, and colleagues often said *no* when I told them that my long-term plans were to perform research or create a career focused on spirituality and science. However, I was fortunate to have wonderful mentors who were constantly encouraging me with the word *yes*. My focus on the positive affirmation and support helped me pursue my personal dreams and interests in forging my career.

So as a doctor who has studied the brain extensively, and its relation to a variety of states from depression to religious ecstasy, I regard the positive emotions of the word *yes* as an absolutely essential part of life and a well-functioning brain.

Part Two

Transformations

Silent Seat

Tosha Silver

When you finally take
your calm and silent seat
on the throne
of your own heart
everything begins
to fall into
its proper place
because
You
Have

Born to Soar

Tara Lemieux

Shrug off the no's—they are temporary. This is your world. In your world there is only yes.

—Jolene Stockman

"*Yes*..." Never before had such a word formed so perfectly against my lips; and leaving to its breath-filled wake, the promise of hope's greatest adventure.

I had lost nearly all connection to yes—struggling through those many years, lost in a relationship that robbed my will in exchange for my love. I had forgotten what it meant to *really* be loved; I had forgotten what it meant to be *me*.

Day after day, I would mourn the beautiful woman I once was: vivacious, sure-footed, and confident beyond measure... with a fearlessness to take on any of life's challenges. Until one day, I found the courage to say "yes" once again.

Yes to this life... *Yes* to my spirit... Why *yes*, even to these torn-up shreds of my most favorite jeans... I found my hope tucked safely within the "looking glass" of my dearest friend, who saw in me that which I have always been: one beautiful human spirit, *undeterred* by the burdens of anyone else's vision.

Isn't it ironic how we must often look so very far *outside* of ourselves to discover this truth *within*? And then one day—by the slightest shift in perspective—the heart becomes our guide, once again. My dears, we were born to be limitless—with dreams crafted upon the billows of darkness, and hope tucked safely 'neath our wings.

We were born to *soar*.

Faith soon displaces doubt's devastation, instilling in us a certain unshakeable knowing. Just as the bird feels the warmth of light, even before the darkness has lifted—still she sings, my dears, she sings with *all* her heart. And in her song, we find the refuge of an unbreakable spirit—valiant in her quest for *carpe diem*. And we too can face each day... courageously perched amongst the tallest of trees, with wings extended and *eager* for flight.

My dears, we were born to live the life we've always dreamed, but never expected. And forgetting to say "*yes*" is the only thing keeping us from it. This one-syllabled gateway between all that we are and all that we might wish to be grants to us our irrefutable *permission to live.*

So find your voice, my dears—step up to your "yes." Say yes to the sunsets... and yes to those rains. And yes to the spirit that carries your dreams. Say yes to that sweet bump in your sashay. And yes to that funky little flip to your hair. Say yes with a boldness you always knew to be there! Say yes to all that you wished for but never quite dared. Say yes to all of it—every single last bit. Go ahead, say yes to the life you were destined to live.

Yes! Me, Myself, and I

Dr. Marissa Pei

Me

A tumultuous relationship with this thing called "ME" defined these past (mumble, mumble) decades. For so long, I danced with codependency, placing everyone else's wishes before my own. I was what they wanted me to be. I wasn't a doormat; I was wall-to-wall carpet. Trying to please the un-pleaseable, I was never happy. When others would tell me how unhappy they were because of me, the criticism worked like a stab in the heart. I felt like a piece of shitake.

I would then swing to the other end of the spectrum and say, "F U, I don't give a flying 'F' through a Rolling Donut what you think. Leave me alone, I'm better than you, so there!" Swinging from "I am hot shitake" to "I am a piece of shitake" extremes resulted in a chronic "dis-ease" with life and self-loathing.

I remember one of my first burning-bush experiences stomping up the stairs after yet another disappointing encounter with my now "wasband," muttering under my breath, "Why doesn't he listen to me? Why doesn't he care about what I want? Why doesn't he respect my desires and feelings?" Burrowed into my bed of self-pity, I suddenly heard a rich, booming voice in my head asking, "What do you want? What are your desires? Do you heed your own voice? Do you listen to yourself?"

Yikes! Thunderstruck, I realized that the problem was with me and the solution was with me as well, not him.

Myself

Throughout my Chinese upbringing I failed again and again when measured against the old saying, "The nail that stands up is hammered down!" When I was being myself, I was accused of being selfish. Any mention of self in a positive way violated the family code of humility. Parents' needs must prevail, or else prepare for a swift slap to the face to mark the end of a long lecture. So I learned very quickly to hide my self, desires, hopes, and dreams behind a thick invisible wall.

I attracted unkind, demanding people and unhealthy relationships until—thanks to many fabulous teachers in my life—I began to care for myself, and was able to peel away the negativity of the "Selfish" label and discover the miracle of who I am and what I want.

& I

Who am I?

Most of us feel like the years of our life go by quickly ... and they do, especially when we are unaware of our own place in it. The most important question I can ask myself to find that place is, "Who am I?"

Many people define themselves in relational terms such as, "I am a mother, a wife, a consultant, a teacher, a friend." And each of them comes with an attachment. Every relational definition comes with requests and expectations from the person we have the relationship with. Many of us recovering perfectionists have a tendency to try to be everything to everybody in every relationship. Instead of focusing on the myriad times we succeed as the good mom/friend/coworker/boss/consultant/singer/writer/actor/sister/wife, unfortunately, we hear criticism, and so we stay on the hamster wheel trying to be perfect. It is exhausting.

So instead, I ask my clients to define themselves in core terms: Are you kind? Generous? Critical? Resourceful? Creative? These core definitions of self are not impacted by a bad day or a bad encounter.

I am eighteen adjectives, and three of them are not very nice. I am positive, enthusiastic, creative, talented, determined, lyrical, expressive, funny, caring, kind, loving, witty, studious, ambitious, fashionable, judgmental, critical, and impatient. When I realized those last three were the very things that I hated about my mother— and I swore I wouldn't be like her—I almost committed *hari-kari*.

Still, I choose to stand in the center of who I am, good and bad. Even having inherited some of my mom's traits, I can be at ease when I cut myself some slack. Of course I am like my mom in some ways. I have her genes. She was my primary role model. Now I am more relaxed about my humanity and embrace my quirky qualities. I love who I am.

Once I am rooted in the core of who I am, I can easily bloom into what I want: the peace that is my birthright. I can breathe into the abundance of a friendly universe and ask for anything that feeds my addiction to joy. My purpose is to be a beneficial presence on the planet, and I believe that I am a unique emanation in the world with gifts, talents, and abilities to express and share, to add to my own happiness. And the secret to my happiness is a beautiful relationship with me, myself, and I, and the Source that created me.

Here's to you saying "yes" to you and yourself! Peace in, and peace out!

Yes to Yes Times Infinity

Daniel Cammarn

Yes to animals. Yes to the plants. Yes to the sun.
Yes to stretching. Yes to the birds in the morning.
Yes to music and losing yourself in someone's word.
Yes to coffee tables. Yes to new life. Yes to your sacrifice.
Yes to your forgiveness. Yes to meeting new people. Yes to
Inspiration. Yes to reading. Yes to free things. Yes to feeling
alive. Yes to running around. Yes to your art. Yes to happy.
Yes to change. Yes to colors. Yes to the crazy things people do.

Yes to Meditation (All of It)

Chris Grosso

It's no secret that the benefits of meditation are more than worth any initial resistance to undertaking the endeavor. I mean, who wouldn't like less stress, lower blood pressure, increased calmness, and greater focus in their daily lives?

For me, however, meditation isn't always blissed-out states of white light and ethereal divine sounds. No, my meditation can be brutal, and I don't mean brutal in the physical sense, like when my knees hurt from sitting for extended periods of time, but rather, brutal in the mental and emotional sense—the place that holds the greatest potential for experiencing pain, where things can get really dark.

The most difficult times I experience in meditation are those that bring up the wreckage of my past actions from my days in active addiction. Violence, blood, broken bones, DUI's, blackouts—and along with those bitter visions comes the pain. My chest tightens, my stomach turns, my fists clench, and my mind churns.

So why do I do it? Why do I stay present with these experiences in meditation when I could escape through distractions? No matter how uncomfortable meditation becomes at times, having experienced the deep solace and burgeoning wisdom through meditation, there is no going back to my old way of life.

It's through learning to sit that I find the strength to feel pain as it arises, to say *yes* to whatever presents itself at that moment, and to allow it rather than running away and numbing myself with drugs. Don't get me wrong—there are some days that still can suck so bad that the idea of quitting tempts me, but these are transformative times. When viewed through eyes of compassion—eyes that see the beauty and Spirit underlying all things and events, no matter how shitty they may appear at face value—my peace deepens. I let go of my past.

Vietnamese monk Thich Nhat Hanh has been quoted as saying, "No mud, no lotus." Life's "mud" is just as valuable as the "lotus." And as I completely open to all of my life, I eventually begin to see that everything is *Spirit-in-action*, which consists of Spirit awakening to more of itself with each unfolding I experience.

A gentle serenity begins to accompany not only the easy times, but the tough ones as well. My experience of equanimity and compassion is no longer reserved strictly for the time I spend on my cushion, but now it accompanies me to my writing desk, to my author interviews, and in the moments I spend with my family and friends.

Through saying yes to everything meditation brings our way, we learn to say yes to life, to fearlessly lay our heart's armor aside and to be more skillful with ourselves, and others. We begin to embody the peace of Buddha, Krishna, Christ, and all of the illumined Ones; and we're sharing it with all sentient beings.

It really is pretty fucking amazing what a simple act of bravery such as sitting down, closing our eyes, and showing up for life can spark.

Watering the Plants

Wayne Lee

It is a simple thing,
watering the household plants.
It can be done without mind.
But then one would miss
drawing the tepid water
from the kitchen faucet,
filling the antique jar,
soaking the soil and feeding
the roots, turning the pots
to meet the sun, spraying
the leaves, breathing in
the perfume of fertility.
All I ask is to be aware.

Pace Is Grace

Jenn Grosso

When I think about what I say yes to, what I try to consciously honor every single day, one word comes to mind: *pace*. I have discovered that when I embrace my own rhythm, this is when I come together with the flow of the universe. I come in touch with my core and unfold from an inner happiness and unending gratitude that isn't easily shaken by day-to-day events. When I let my life expand without struggle, I can truly be myself and allow my gifts to shine through. This is Grace.

Sounds easy enough, doesn't it? In my experience, however, I see the grace of pace often clouded by my expectations, by comparing myself to others, by buying into the thoughts that I should be doing more, being more, and achieving more. That I should be writing more, contributing more, making more art, getting out there more. On that cycle, the sweetness of the graceful unfolding turns sour.

But then I remember that every moment is an opportunity to say yes to my own pace. It's taken me time—through observation, meditation, and cultivating compassion toward myself—to fully appreciate and cherish the gifts that pace has to offer. For me these gifts have shown up as peace within, a trust in myself, and finding such a joy in my own rhythm that the road is smoother, and life more vibrant.

It's not about being perfect and never faltering, but when I say yes to my own pace, to however much time I need, the barriers dissolve. I feel free and completely a part of everything, where all things click effortlessly into alignment. And my actions come right from my heart center. I have found that if I honor and embrace my own stride, then everything else seems to fall into place. Pace is indeed Grace.

Life's Sweet Honey

Faith Keolker

Just as the first bee
sets out from its hive
in Spring and is drawn
to the pollen of a flower—
even as it is buffeted and
pressed by the wind—so it is
that we find our way to that
which we truly believe.

Rewired

Rose Caiola

As a child, I always believed in happiness, a better way to be. There were times when I was profoundly unhappy, but even then I knew something better was possible.

There was nobody to blame for my troubles—that's just the way life is. We're all products of our environments. Our parents didn't have the awareness we have today, and neither did theirs. My mother and father didn't know there was such a thing as ADHD and just thought I was lazy. *Their* parents lived in a village in Sicily with no running water or telephones, where they owned and operated a flourmill—backbreaking work—so things like learning disabilities, therapy, and intentional parenting weren't part of their reality. But each generation is given more tools and it's our responsibility to use them.

I was the youngest of three children, the unplanned, unwanted daughter, referred to as "the accident." I wasn't supposed to happen. And I began to believe that I was a burden, which fostered feelings of unworthiness. For most of my adolescence, I searched outside myself in all the usual ways—substances, relationships, accomplishments—but never quite found what I was looking for. It wasn't until I was almost an adult—nineteen—that I first said *yes* to my positive intuitions, and began the rewiring journey that I'm still on today.

You may be wondering what I mean by *rewiring*.

Basically it's unlearning all the misconceptions I was taught growing up. Rewiring is a process of *expressing, sharing, embracing,* and *living*—of saying yes to life's possibilities! (And if you're reading this book of inspiration and insight, you're probably pretty open to the idea.)

I had gotten to the point where whenever I felt an unpleasant emotion, I couldn't deal with it so I'd find someone to blame, as if someone else were responsible for making me feel that way. It was safer to acknowledge and talk to my friends about superficial emotions, avoiding the more painful underlying ones. I used to get stuck in the "poor me" syndrome. I'd blame my unhappiness on everyone else, never thinking the source could have come from within. That would have been too much to bear!

My rewiring began with expression—connecting with the emotions that were at the root of my unhappiness. In order to do that, I had to get help. I found a therapist (who is still my mentor twenty years later). Our work together helped me dig deep and peel away the layers around my discomfort—revealing anger I'd turned into sadness, and sadness into worthlessness. Expressing my feelings of being unworthy brought me a sense of peace—when I felt safe to feel my emotions, they lost their power over my mind and heart. In other words, I had taken a step toward saying *yes* to rewiring.

Expressing and sharing gave me the strength to embrace and overcome life's challenges and say *yes* to my whole self, feelings and all. Saying *yes* has helped me become stronger, happier, more peaceful, and a better person all around. True happiness and inner peace are our psychological and spiritual birthright. We're born into this life in our purest form: no judgment, no opinions, no attachments. Aren't we meant to be happy and free? It's there in all of us and, when we claim it, we are free to live a life of *yes*—and it's a beautiful life!

Feeling worthy of life has changed me in a big way. I've come to really like who I am. It's helped me choose who I want to spend my time with and uncover who I want to be. When I'm the "real Rose" with people, "real" people appear in my life and we communicate on deeper, more meaningful levels and this contributes to my happiness over and over again.

I started my website Rewire Me because I was given a gift. Life presented me with an opportunity to grow, to go through this process of express, share, embrace, and live—and I accepted it. My heart is full of love and gratitude every day, and I want others to experience this because everyone deserves a chance to love themselves and everyone deserves a chance to be happy—to say yes!

Vital Yes

Linda Thompson Whidby

Saying no was killing me.

My soul wanted my attention. Ignoring it spun me into a numb apathy of depression. My refusal to listen left me anxious, drained, and hopeless. I used addictions to food, shopping, and sex to suffocate my dreams. I sought cold comfort in anything outside of myself, running away from the poems and stories that longed to be expressed, and from the beginning of my sacred inner exploration.

I did not understand the language of my most vital force. I believed that serenity was found in security and control and acquiring stuff. *If I can just hang on long enough, everything will be okay.* I employed myriad delay tactics to avoid my childhood dream of writing. *I will write when I retire, when I have the perfect creative space, when I lose enough weight, when I get out of debt, when I become successful, when my kids are grown.* That precious part of me—my intuition— could not reach me. I had cut it off. Like a decapitated snake, my body writhed and squirmed without direction.

Everything changed when I began to listen to my heart's guidance, to nurture myself, and to explore my creative power. I trusted my inner voice, which spoke with unmistakable clarity, quitting a job that drained me. I have since enjoyed the past three years unmedicated, loving the aspects of myself I formerly hated, and letting go of the knife—forged in fear and tempered with shame—that I had held against my own spirit. How good it feels to say yes to my soul's sweetest impulse!

Saying *yes* saved my life and it changed the way I conduct it. Now I live effortlessly. Friends, opportunities, and miracles show up with staggering ease and consistency. Acceptance, serenity, and peace define my days. Force is no longer required to accomplish my visions. Relationships no longer require work. Patterns of addiction and codependency dissolve. Balance prevails.

I have learned that becoming a writer is as simple as *being* a writer. My spirit knows my worthiness moment by moment, and wants me to trust it to communicate what brings me joy. My dream of writing springs from that vitality. It was here all along whispering to me, ready to be born. Now, unafraid of any feeling that arises, I step out of my own way and write. I follow the subtle inner prompts toward joy. I say yes to my soul's guidance; I say yes to my vital force; I say yes to my divine prescription.

Part Three

Creativity

Your Evolving Soul Is Happy to Say Yes

Brandi Leigh Whitehead

Say Yes with finesse, your evolving soul with inspiration and goals
Accessing playfulness, possess the craziness, dizziness with joyfulness
Let it roll, you as a whole nothing controls, worldliness as you say yes
Joyfulness from no bitterness, ongoing foolishness
Embracing youthfulness with grand wishfulness
Appears like you're on a playground at recess
Always to inspire with carefreeness, the options are limitless
Outrageously seen dangerously penniless,
But truly not under duress, barely escaping the eeriness,
True happiness is your evolving soul's willingness,
to say YES!

Yes! And...

Liz Alexander, Ph.D.

Had anyone asked, I'm sure each of us would have described ourselves as positive, accepting, can-do people. Once onstage, the evidence suggested otherwise. We were thwarting in a way that my school lacrosse coach would have been proud of. Only in this case, success meant prematurely and selfishly curtailing "the game."

Some weeks earlier, I'd been gifted the book *Improv Wisdom: Don't Prepare, Just Show Up*, by Patricia Ryan Madson. Given the way that coincidences often compound, a client of mine had also recently shared her concept of "a fear a year." That triggered my interest in doing something I'd never tried before: three months of improvised comedy classes, an idea that both excited and terrified me.

My motive for going ahead was fueled by an interest in embracing a new, "foreign" skill, learning how to be consciously funny, and perhaps enjoying being around people who also loved the idea of "playtime for grown-ups." But the terror twin loomed large, too. Certainly I'm no shy, retiring type. And professionally, I'm well used to making presentations—often extemporaneously—in front of complete strangers. But that's when I'm offering up material that is as much a part of me as my DNA. Sharing a stage with folks I needed to *rely on*, in front of an audience expecting us to *amuse them*, without a script or even much of an idea of what was *supposed to happen*, seemed beyond the pale to me. What was left to do but sign up?

"Yes" is the foundational precept of improv. As Madson describes it, "The world of yes may be the single most powerful secret of improvising." Our workshop instructor compellingly explained why: "Yes" is expansive, while "No" shrinks your options as surely as wool clothing in a hot dryer. With that piece of wisdom under our wings, we were set loose on our first practice exercise. Two people crept onto the stage. One was to offer the opening line "Let's plan a party," and the other would respond positively. Simple enough, right? Yet here's what happened:

Lisa: Let's plan a party.

Jude: Why don't we go out for Chinese instead?

(At this point, imagine the jarring sound of a game show buzzer.)

Stop right there, our workshop facilitator and experienced improviser admonished. Seems we'd just seen what improvisers call "blocking," which directly contradicted what the exercise required: accepting the gift to kick-start the process of creation. The participants were to try again with a little more enthusiasm and follow each prompt with a statement, not a question:

Lisa: Let's plan a party!

Jude: Yes!!!! We can go out for Chinese and talk about it then.

(Game show buzzer.)

The two volunteers looked at each other sheepishly. What had they done wrong now? Well, we'd heard "Yes," followed by an unspoken "But." This was a subtle yet invidious way of shutting down the conversation by suggesting that the gift was unworthy or unwelcome. Accept the gift (say yes), then build on it (and ...):

Lisa: Let's plan a party!!

Jude: Yes. And we can invite everyone from our improv group.

Lisa: Yes. And ask them to dress like it's the 1960s.

Jude: Yes. And also bring a poem, a song, or a piece of art that was created by someone they admire from that era.

Lisa: Yes. And then we can decorate the venue with all their ideas.

Jude: Yes. And use that material as prompts for some improvised games.

This went on for some time, like an equally matched tennis game. Which turned into a satisfying-to-watch, nail-biting back-and-forth, meandering into often hilarious and always interesting new territory. After all, the gift offered up by the party suggestion was just a prelude to co-creating something *more*.

What other options involving yes had we still not covered, our instructor wanted to know? The clever kid in the room's hand shot up: "Why not just say 'Yes' and leave it at that?" Two new volunteers stepped up onstage to give it a try.

Angela: Let's plan a party!!!

Josh: Yes, I like that idea.

Angela: Yes! And we can book that new venue down by the river.

Josh: Yep. Sounds like fun.

Angela: Yes. And we can have the cupcake people cater.

Josh: Oh, yes, I love cupcakes.

This continued in the same vein for several minutes, concluded by the sound of Angela's deep sigh. She said the exercise had felt frustrating and exhausting. Why? Because from her perspective, she appeared to be the only person doing any *offering*; her partner just sucked up her ideas as efficiently as a vacuum cleaner, while showing as much interest in giving any real input as an inanimate object. That was the problem with saying "yes" without "and."

We recapped: In order to be a conscious creator, you first need to accept the gift—the "offer," in improv parlance—and be aware that even an innocuous line like "Let's plan a party" isn't prescriptive. If you are so controlling as to only run with your own ideas ("Why don't we go out for Chinese instead?"), then you'll likely miss the *possibilities* that hide like matryoshka dolls inside the gift.

How often are we even consciously aware of life's offerings or believe we are saying yes, yet with the resistance of an unspoken "but"? By saying "Yes! And..." we are, as Madson explains in *Improv Wisdom*, supporting our own or someone else's dreams. I believe there's more to it than that because we're helping transport those dreams further than originally thought possible. "Yes! And..." is the secret sauce of conscious creation (ergo improvised success), not just an enthusiastic, resounding "Yes."

All of which makes perfect sense to me, given how my life has shaped up. If Helen Keller hadn't gotten there first, I would have wanted to write the line, "Life is either a daring adventure or nothing." I'm an unabashed "Yes! And..." person. I stepped into my dream life as a mega-selling nonfiction author back in the late 1980s, with no platform and no agent, after receiving a yes to my first manuscript from a London publisher. I experienced a long-held desire to become a BBC presenter after first saying yes to a local cable TV opportunity. I enjoyed a satisfying and lucrative 20-year career as a freelance journalist (without even an undergraduate degree at that point, let alone one in journalism) when I said yes to writing my first few articles for free. I gained a Master's and a Ph.D. in educational psychology, despite having been out of mainstream education for almost 40 years, and parlayed both achievements into my business—which has nothing to do with education or psychology *per se*.

Life has presented me—as it does to each one of us, every single day—with offers to which I gladly said yes without concerning myself with whether I was qualified, worthy, or might end up falling flat on my face. Then I *added* to each opportunity in order to craft a unique and fulfilling life.

While I'm all in favor of "yes," I remain wary of where it—alone—can take us. Consider the danger to our innate creativity from the "yeses" we don't even think about. Like allowing computer algorithms to choose the same kinds of books, music, or other intellectual and artistic pleasures for us. Amazon makes recommendations, and by saying yes to them, we're actually saying no to thinking for ourselves and making choices that stretch beyond long-established boundaries. And when we only listen to or watch channels that support our existing political beliefs, aren't we really shutting out other perspectives and points of view? In each of these cases we're saying yes, but at the risk of holding our lives static, frozen, *bereft*.

Arguably there is no greater exemplar of "Yes! And…" than founding father Benjamin Franklin, whose curiosity puts him at the top of my list of polymaths, certainly. Here was a man who didn't just say yes to his country as a politician but added to the richness of his life as an author, businessman, inventor, and scientist. Rather than confining himself to one role, he enhanced each individual contribution by embracing multiple opportunities to serve. He lived *additively*.

Long-term heroine of mine Dame Anita Roddick founded The Body Shop (now an international brand owned by L'Oréal) in 1976 with no business training or any experience making beauty products. She didn't just say yes to entrepreneurialism, but added a chorus of glorious, important ands: That a company selling pots of nice-smelling creams could take a stand on human rights; that it had a responsibility to be environmentally friendly; that a high-profile business leader could (and should) lend her name and clout to important political issues like poverty and global warming.

And George R. R. Martin, the *Game of Thrones* storyteller, didn't say yes to writing fantasy novels like J. R. R. Tolkien—he made the genre his own. His "Yes! And…" involved killing off key characters at unexpected junctures, incorporating true-to-life elements of political intrigue, and creating characters who occupy that more realistic realm we call "gray" because they're capable of both good *and* evil.

A truly mouthwatering, luscious life isn't about saying yes if that only means "good enough," "granted," "naturally," "unquestionably," or "undoubtedly." It's about saying "Yes! And…" because that's how we best create our unique adventure playgrounds.

Will you join us?

Commuter's Ballet

Kathy McGrath

YES! To Amazing Grace! How Sweet the Sound
This song claims to save wretches like me
But, I've lifted out. I'm not a wretch
I never was and never will be.
In fact, I've no need to be saved
YES! I am a Supreme Being
Who loves to
Sing Amazing Grace my Way!
4am: YES! Amazing Grace is staring back at me when I look in the
mirror
Amazing Grace is quiet moments in my car
5:30am: YES! As my snow-tired little car that could and does
Get me to the train station … one more precious hour to work
6am: Amazing Grace is on the train
Amazing Grace is the beautiful Urban Ballet during my commute
YES! I'm the STAR dancer bundled and warm
Shuffling quickly to work, to home
Masses of Supreme Beings Crisscrossing in a Graceful Urban Ballet
YES!—We are Amazing Grace!
Grace floats and blows down from the heavens
Softly Landing on my Nose. And lips and tongue and eyelashes.
7am: YES! Amazing Grace as the Urban Ballet Star makes it to
work
CHICAGO! CHICAGO ! My kind of town
YES! To every precious graceful moment …
YES! To Amazing Grace!

Notes from a Cowgirl Guru

Lola Jones

God

Someone asked me, "Why did you write a humor book when you're known worldwide for serious spiritual books?"

Because God told me to, silly. Even told me to call it *Confessions of a Cowgirl Guru.*

God said, "Lola, you've got more energy than a 1950s housewife on diet pills. Here's another project for you: please, please help bring some levity to the way, way, way too serious spiritual world.

"The only people who will talk to me are the spiritual people, and they are so freakin' serious. The sinners would be way more fun to talk to, but they don't speak to me at all. Oh, sure, they holler when they're in trouble, but how much fun is that for me?

"That over-seriousness is a giant speed bump on the path to enlightenment. Please, tell them it's called en-lighten-ment, not enheavy-ment. We'd all be having a lot more fun if you spiritual folk down there would chill out and lighten up.

"You're running around seeking Me, reading all these books, listening to channelers, attending all these seminars, looking everywhere but inside yourselves. Hello-oo! I'm right here!"

I agree with God. Stereotypes are silly, and it's even sillier when people follow them rather than being who they really are. I don't want to look, sound, act, think, or operate like a stereotypical spiritual teacher—boring! I'm a cowgirl from Texas who happily transplanted herself, and her horses, to California soil.

I've painted erotic paintings as often as spiritual ones, and written some erotic fiction.

Mom was visiting and observed, "You have paintings of naked butts all over your house."

I said, "Mom—I know that." She wanted prints.

When a group of new people are getting to know each other I like to playfully get them to guess each other's profession. People often guess that my boyfriend, Russell, is a writer—that's an easy one—he just looks like a writer! It's more fun to watch them scrunch up their face and try to guess mine. I'll prod, "Okay, what are you thinking, retired pole dancer turned interior decorator?"

No one ever guesses me right. I don't fit the stereotype of a spiritual teacher. A voluptuous blonde wearing fashionable clothes or cowgirl garb doesn't typically suggest spiritual teacher. No white robes or prayer beads for me—those things make me look fat!

While having lunch with a women's networking group, Penny, a friend of mine, heard someone mention my name. She kept quiet as a mouse and straight-faced as a moose while they gossiped.

Then one of them commented with a slight smirk, "Yeah, Lola Jones. I looked up her website. She's the Marilyn Monroe of spiritual teachers."

Penny said to me, "I decided it was time for me to pipe up, so I offered, 'Yes, isn't she cool? She's so different. Lola is one of my best friends!'" The woman changed the subject pretty quickly as Penny grinned a huge, evil grin.

They didn't know the half of it: In my younger days I was in the *Playboy* Magazine issue "The Girls of John Deere."

I've told my sweetheart, Russell: If you ever see me wearing white robes, speaking in hushed, reverent tones, acting all spiritual and crap, get a gun (if you happen to be in Texas, where I'm from, anybody will happily lend you one), shoot me on the spot, and throw my body to the coyotes.

I was serious. Just that once. But don't expect much of that from here on out.

Mom

Guns ... that reminds me of my mom.

My mother is funny: Patsy Ernestine Wacky Jones. Her whole family was hilarious, but she has the bonus gift of being funny when she doesn't know she's being funny—until you start laughing, then she gets it and starts laughing.

One November she inquired in her sweet drawl, "Lola, you have everything—I just don't know what to get you for Christmas, and with you living alone out there on those ten acres—would you like a gun?"

She was perfectly serious. I tried to keep a straight face. I did. I tried.

"Mom, that is so sweet—so much in the spirit of Christmas! I'd think of you every time I got to shoot somebody." Then she laughed.

She didn't give up, though. Another Christmas she asked, "OK, if you don't want a gun—how about a stun gun?"

Lola, Are You in a Cult?

After my relatives read my serious spiritual book, *Things Are Going Great in My Absence*, which didn't sound anything like the Bible, they earnestly discussed the fate of my soul, worried that God was going to smite me.

Mom, with great concern, eventually was the one who approached me, completely failing her attempt not to sound accusatory despite the sweet accent:

"Lola-sweethawt, are you in a cult?"

Struggling to maintain a straight face, I basked in the glee of what I was about to say. Mom leaned forward.

It was one of those moments when angels sang "Aaaahhhh," as I channeled the great masters of humor; the perfect reply prepared to spring from my full, quivering, Jezebel lips.

"MOOOooommmmmMMM," I whined, "I can't believe you would even ask me a question like that! Am I in a cult? A cult? Do you think I'm a sheep? Don't you know me any better than that? I am NOT in a cult...! I'm LEADING a cult!"

She almost fell over laughing, and she never mentioned it again. She read my book (yes, it's serious, and yes, it works) and now brags about me to everyone, "You should see my daaaw-ah-tuuuh riding her hawuus. She lives in that fine hay-uus on that heee-ull in Cali-faw-nee-uh."

41

Lick Here

People used to call me at odd hours from across the world until I became more well known and had to take my phone number off my website. Two young guys called me at 11 p.m. one night—they were flirting and having fun, and did not seem to be sincerely interested in my work or my books at all. I answered their questions and they giggled until the call ended, leaving me mystified as to why they had phoned.

Later, on a hunch, I checked out the page on my website about my book on dating that the callers had mentioned. My picture is on the image of the book cover. The link should have said, "To find out more, or to order, click on the book cover above." But apparently I had accidentally deleted one letter in the link one day while I was tweaking the copy, so it said in huge letters right on the cover over my face:

"To find out more, or to order, lick here."

I laughed till my stomach hurt and called up three friends to share.

In that pathetic, aging way, I'm actually grateful that young guys would still bother to call me in the middle of the night. A few years ago, guys twenty years younger than I am, who used to flirt with me, started calling me Ma'am.

Ma'am? This was horrifying. "Pardon me, young man," I'd say, "Don't call me Ma'am!" They'd be embarrassed and say, "My mom taught me to say that, sorry, Ma'am, uh. ... I mean, sorry."

It was the end of an era. Now if a young guy is staring at me, I probably have spinach in my teeth or else he's lusting after my Mac-Book Pro laptop.

They're too young to remember Marilyn Monroe, so being the Marilyn Monroe of spiritual teachers doesn't get me a damn thing.

OK, gotta go now—a new idea for a song is playing in my head. It may be spiritual or it may end up punkabilly—I love writing and recording music in many styles! We'll see what the muses bring me next.

I always say YES to inspiration.

Creativity: The Heart of the Matter

Sally King

Creativity has its source in the life force that comes from within. It is a living energy that swirls and spirals, gathering momentum as it does. It is a vibrant, positive energy and yet, like a hurricane, it can be destructive if not channeled appropriately. We all have innate creativity: it is the force by which we can express our inner nature, be it artistically, musically, or physically—but it must be expressed. Otherwise that creative force builds and builds like a storm creating its own path without direction.

Nature illustrates to us the power of creativity every day. We see its magically transforming energy in the changing seasons and the dying orange embers of a beautiful dusk's retreat. We observe the sunset as the colours and shifting clouds change with such alacrity that the canvas of the sky is a new painting every second. Creativity is the energy of the universe and all of nature; it is the heart of our matter.

The creative force of pure energy within us—if expressed—can lead to harmony and an incredible sense of joy and peace, the power of which can sometimes feel overwhelming. It is our avenue to Spirit; it is our road to completeness. And yet how many of us express our genius? Many of us sit on it, deny it, and ignore its call, drowning it out with our busy lives until eventually it drowns us with its demands. Like holding back the river, sitting on our creative energy can deplete our bodies of vitality. I have noticed over the years that if I have a period of time when I do not act on my creative callings, I not only feel an irrational level of irritation but also a debilitating whole-body lethargy. Unacknowledged and unexpressed creativity can lead to depression and illness. We cannot deny a living energy for long, and if we don't give it a channel it will find its own.

Creativity demands of us that we give it attention so it can grow, but we must also remember to be gentle and patient with creativity's timing. I grow orchids at home in the English Cotswolds. I have always loved their delicacy and beauty, and I find them the easiest of houseplants to grow. I am constantly delighted by their presence in my home. When the flowers eventually die away, I trim them back and leave them for a period of rest in a warm spot with some light, taking care to water them a touch every two weeks. Each one of them takes their own period of time to grow back. Some send a new shoot up instantly, and some take months but they always do return, their flowers multiplying every time.

One of my favourite pink orchids is doing just that at the moment, its tiny buds slowly opening to reveal the most beautiful petals. If you watch closely you can almost see them opening. I was observing them a few days ago, sitting with my pink orchid, reveling in nature's ability to refresh and renew from seemingly nowhere, when I noticed one of the buds wasn't opening. It looked as though the petals had fused shut, so I took hold of the bud and gently prised apart the petals to allow it to open freely.

The next day I came downstairs eager to see this beautiful flower fully revealed only to find that it was wilting off the stalk, totally lifeless, all of its colour having drained away. I was distraught and wondered if the whole plant was dying, so over the next few days I simply observed it. What I found was that as each flower opened, it went through a stage when the petals appeared to experience the same challenge of sticking together until eventually they opened with a flourish. The bud that I had helped to open had by this point fallen off. It was then that I understood. If I had left that bud to its own devices and not interfered with the very natural process that was occurring, it would have opened perfectly well by itself, having built strength from its struggle to open. Because I did the work for it, it did not get a chance to build that essential strength, and it died.

Our gift is at the heart of our creativity and our creativity is at the heart of who we are. Those who are happiest are those who know themselves, acknowledge their gift, and are able to overcome self-imposed barriers in order to share it.

Poet Samuel Taylor Coleridge said, "what comes from the heart, goes to the heart." When we speak from the heart, it rings clearly in the hearts of others. It is that which resonates with us in a book, a song, a poem, or even a newspaper article. It speaks to us of our shared inheritance: our desire to create and to appreciate creation. So, it behooves us as creators to find our heart's song, and to create from that voice. In this way, creativity is a means of communicating from heart to heart.

It was this very topic I was questioning while I wandered into a pottery shop in a tiny hilltop town in southern Tuscany. It was bliss escaping the blinding heat of the cobbled streets, and I paused in the cool, dark cavern watching the potter create. At once I was struck by his attention to his work, as if his entire being was consumed by the task. He had a deftness of touch that was inspiring, and as the soft clay changed shape in his hands, it was as though a small miracle was taking place. There were shelves and shelves of his work crowding the tiny shop, each creation displayed with the same meticulous attention to detail to show off its best aspect under the lights. I was mesmerised by what seemed like pure alchemy: the ability to take a piece of rough-hewn clay and transform it into a stunning shapely azure-blue vase.

On the counter I found and purchased a book written by the potter himself, Franco Balducci. In this beautifully scribed and illustrated book, Franco describes his reflections on the art of throwing a pot and how that skill so brilliantly mirrors our quest to find our own centre and create from it. The contents of that little book were so vital to me at that time, it was as if God had led me directly to the answers to my questions. For days I pored over that little book and absorbed what the potter was telling me, each line compelling me toward a greater understanding about the truth of creativity. I learnt that the potter cannot throw a good pot without first finding the centre of the clay, a skill which in itself can take a lifetime of practice. If a potter attempts to make a pot without this vital element, the pot goes floppy and collapses. Once the centre is found, it is then up to the potter to create what he desires.

From the centre, all things are possible and there are no boundaries, less the imagination of the creator. The centre represents the umbilical connection to creativity, the place from which that spark of inspiration can be born: the fertile void. Between the potter's hands and the clay, a design can be moulded to a plan or become a free expression that takes form without planning. Going with the flow of the wheel and the feel of the clay, spontaneous forms can appear and often they can be the most successful. But the clay cannot be moulded if the wheel is not turning, and it is the potter who turns the wheel at the pace he desires—he is in control. Potting requires the centrifugal force the turning of the wheel creates, just like our universe holds us in the world of gravity.

Interestingly, once the pot is created, painted, and fired, the centre of the pot transforms from being the umbilical connection to the spark of creativity, to being an empty space, a void. Once the pot sits on the potter's shelf, it becomes a vessel, full of space, full of nothing. I know from my own meditation, my own connection to my larger self, that when I am connected, the peace of nothingness is all-embracing. That is my centre, the truth of who I am and the centre of all things, physical and nonphysical.

We are the potters of our lives. We can create, we can move, we can change, we can assume our power, and we can choose love. We are the centrifugal force, the wheel, the clay, and the pot, and when we are connected to our true selves, we can shift the universe.

Creativity lives in and through us. It really is at the heart of our matter. It only requires one thing of us and that is to say yes! The power of saying yes throws open our hearts and minds to new possibilities. If we say yes with our heart, our soul, our presence, our attention, and our breath, then we say yes to ourselves, to life, and to all that we can create.

Inception: Yes to the Muse

Joanne S. Bodin

It's a tiny drop of dew on a blade of grass after a rainstorm

that won't let you shift your focus until it burrows into your

   subconscious

with tangled images that call out to you

then it disappears for awhile

but you know it's still there, the melancholy thoughts

still disjointed, pulling at you to give them life

to tell their story until they weigh you down with abandon

you try to convince yourself that it's not your story

but then the tidal wave envelopes your subconscious

and debris of human suffering wash along

the shore of your mind and interrupt your everyday routine

then it disappears for awhile

until you are sitting at the Sixth Street Cafe with your writing pad

cup of Moroccan dark roast coffee

the sound of rain pellets on the picture window

in the corner of your wooden booth

the drone of a train whistle tunnels into your subconscious

synapses begin firing away

a train roars by

rain mixed with snow blurs your vision

you look out of the window

see the ghostly shadow of the red caboose as it disappears into the
    mist

suddenly the fog lifts

you see distant sun drenched fields of poppies and columbine

the entire story now unfolds and you know everyone so well

their stature, their favorite foods, their deepest secrets

and your hand begins to write

you dribble words onto paper like creamy butterscotch candy

in metaphors of longing, of pain and euphoria

that dance with you in a tango of sentences

the floodgates, now open

you stay with them till the finish, not to win the race

but to honor their presence

and the heaviness lifts

your muse gives you a creative wink

and runs off to romp in her fields of glory

When I Grow Up

Karen McSwain

A few weeks ago, I attended something called a "renegade show," which, like all forms of free entertainment, contained a compelling mix of pure talent and painful displays of unabashed self-promotion. People performed magic tricks and graceful acts of aerial acrobatics. A man recited a poem that included the refrain, "Her wings went limp when he pierced her." Someone tamed an imaginary lion.

The event took place in a barn, and many of the onlookers were hippies clad in musty, rumpled garments, their thick, "white-people dreads" splayed across their backs like botched taxidermy. There were very few chairs, so most of the audience sat cross-legged on the floor. I had the misfortune of positioning myself next to a man whose feet smelled as if he had just walked several miles with his boots full of cheese. In this gathering of eccentrics, I stood out, simply because of my mediocrity: a middle-aged woman in black, sporting blue eyeliner and a bob.

I've always been uncomfortable in groups—there, but not fully revealed, the human version of an echo or an underwater scream. My special talent is my ability to notice and not be noticed, which is a fine skill to have if you're an assassin… or a writer. Words are my closest allies and my most prized possessions. Thoughts and phrases reveal themselves to me over time, word by word, in tattered notebooks, or on scraps of paper that flutter from my purse unbidden when I'm rooting around in search of loose change or a tampon.

My words are meant for paper, not ears.

I live in close proximity to a liberal arts college, in a town populated with artsy, creative people, so my world is rife with opportunities to attend "renegade shows," book talks, and poetry readings.

Occasionally, I am even invited to read something that I've written (aloud—to a room full of other living, breathing humans) and I am immediately overcome with a paralyzing fear. I want so badly to do it, but I always decline because I can't shake the humiliating vision of myself standing before my peers, clutching a sweat-dampened piece of notebook paper, mute and frozen.

I recently attended a fiftieth birthday celebration for a friend who is a bona fide writer. Her birthday wish was to surround herself with other writers on her special night and have them read pieces of their work aloud. The small venue where the party took place quickly filled up with poets, fiction writers, and lyricists eager to share their beautiful words. I really wanted to read a poem for my friend, but instead, I lurked in a corner and consumed my body weight in Little Smokies, while a woman I had never met before told me about her former crack addiction.

Just yesterday, I was hanging out in my favorite local coffee shop, doing what I do: writing quietly in a corner, and observing a bunch of guys with names like Cedar, Aspen, and Forrest, as they talked excitedly about the upcoming Procession of the Species parade. I imagined they were the millennial generation's version of the Wonder Twins, and willed them to stand in a circle and join hands, hoping they might unwittingly conjure a cabin. My reverie was broken when a little girl in oversized rubber boots plopped down on the bench next to me and started talking.

Her name was Gaia, and she proceeded to tell me about all of the things she was harboring in her shiny pink backpack. Then she scooted closer, glanced over at my notebook, and asked me what I was doing.

Me: "I'm writing a story."

Gaia: "What's it called?"

Me: "When I Grow Up, I Want to Be a Writer."

Gaia (putting her chubby little hand in mine): "Will you read it to me?"

For Writers

Maureen Buchanan Jones

Go ahead, put it down.
Your pen won't cringe.

Your paper won't shudder.
Go ahead, start the ink.
Follow it to the bottom
of the page.

You'll find it there.
It's waiting,
patient and unafraid.
It holds something

you've been wanting.

It's yours.
It is the most perfect thing

about you.
Go ahead,
take the Yes.

Part Four

All Is Welcome Here

Lightning

Tosha Silver

When I finally said

Yes

the sky cracked open
diamonds fell

on treetops

I gave up

no more
bargaining

no more
demands

You clapped

lightning

pierced the darkness

just Yes
and Yes
and Yes
and Yes

Unshackled

Tosha Silver

When you let
the Divine take
the lead

old desires
begin to
hatch

and be fulfilled

anyway

(as a gift
from Love
Herself)

except
now

you're not
their
slave.

Spirit Garden

Doreen Perrine

What's the question? Something I'd avoid if asked?
How can I answer a question that posits either melodrama or
    age-old nothingness?
Yes to me? Yes to mindset? To menopause? Yes to my Kwan Yin,
the goddess who evokes a "yes" no matter how I come to her;
    kneeling, crawling;
seated lotus style, mudra-fingered, and awaiting a goddess-worthy
    answer?

Silent yes is an evocation of growth to life come to blossom in my
    spirit garden.
Fill in the blank answer with color; gloss it with shimmering blue
    woven between bare trees.
Clouds float in disarray, but I make an otherworldly connection
    anyway.
Yes to my unanswered questions tossed onto a path that tumbles
    across land to never-ending water, sky, air.
Say yes to Earth who needs us, not on bended knees or crawling
    reverse-evolution on all fours,
but upright with arms and hearts spread to take on the restoration
    at hand.

Y

Dominique Mazeaud

I have fallen for a letter, you know, that little squiggle with a trunk and two branches... *Yes, Y*... a small replica of her mother tree. I call *Y* my familiar. Our relationship goes back ten years, when I began picking up the forked branches Nature generously sprinkles on the mountain paths blessing my life in New Mexico. Over time, I discovered *Y* stood for things that are truly me. Praise (a *YES* in raised arms). Divination (a *YES* for the water world). Pilgrim (a *YES* carrying my pilgrimage bundle).

To keep in her company, I hang around words that wear her colors, words like *Yes, Yearning, mYsterY*... The result: *Y* teaches me to *flY*... Like everything in Nature, she is one emissary speaking a language I understand. No philosophical treatise necessary, only the most beautiful wisdom, all about the extraordinary in the ordinary. Here is what several fellow beings taught me during a Buddhist retreat at the Vallecitos Mountain Refuge, and these were not the formal "teachers."

*

One free hour between breakfast and the second meditation session of the day gave me the chance to revisit Icarus, the single-name appellation listed as one of the many possible hikes in this wondrous 9,000-foot-high refuge.

If you had followed me up the hill, you would have felt the awe that made me want to tiptoe all the way. You would have noticed the forest's density... a welcome change from New Mexican sparse reality, a pocket of rich wildness speaking mYsterY. At the same

time, you may, like me, have felt aroused with … well … a bit of ap-
prehension. Then, after a last steep incline, together we would have
reached Icarus. Once there, you, too, would not know what to marvel at, the vista or the work of art.

Walking sticks assisted my steps on the bumpy path, thick grass-
es tingling with morning dew. After startling a family of geese out of
the neighboring pond, I reached the barbed wire gate on which hung
a sign announcing that I was leaving the refuge "at my own risk."
Indeed, I had entered a kind of *terra incognita*: trees, mostly pines,
abounded, a lush undergrowth blanketed the ground, and rocky out-
croppings, stretching their cubical hands, overshadowed the path.

Soon after I began my journey, alternating my gaze between
looking down at the path so as not to stumble and looking ahead to
see where I was going, I caught sight of something flashing ahead …
a furry back undulating in between a tree cluster, reddish like a fox's.
My heart jumped. A mountain lion, the sublime cat also known as
predator to high-country wanderers? Soon the shadow of my fear
lifted to acknowledge the blessing that this mini pilgrimage meant
to me.

A few more steps, something else in the *uncanny* category caught
my attention. At first, I could not determine if it was arboreal or animal. It definitely was a living creature, about three feet tall, erect on
its hind legs in the middle of the path, its body encircled by mane-
like hair ranging from brown to gray to white.

A porcupine!

I knew it was not a hedgehog, the like of which I remember seeing once upon a time along a road in France. I stopped and stared at
the apparition the way the haloed creature seemed to be staring at
me. Soon, its little arm-paws went down and it shuffled away toward
a hollow trunk lying nearby. Walking backward, I resumed my journey, holding my gaze in the direction of the porcupine. Interestingly,
I did not notice any barbed quills. What struck me was that it did not
seem to be bothered by my presence.

The eerie creature had placed itself on a leveled area, a few feet
ahead of the last climb that would bring me to my destination. Because of the determined position, as well as its disheveled appear-
ance, also my inclination for the mythic, this "it" became a "she."
Yes, this being could well pass for an old hag, an odd-looking fairy

queen of the forest. It's not that I ever thought she'd eat me up the way *Hansel and Gretel's* hag is known to have planned; rather, there was some encompassing message in her apparition … a lingering feeling of something special … something potentially tender … a soft wind speaking to my soul …

Nature's wise voice abounds. With the presence of mind we were cultivating in the retreat, it was easy to notice this Mother's infinite ingenuity, the manner in which she takes every opportunity to teach. Earlier in the week, crickets and hummingbirds, from the meadow classrooms surrounding the meditation lodge, had spoken to me.

The lesson had something to do with flYing. We are animals, after all, evolved from fish to bird to mammal. For us human animals, the question may be to live with such ease that we appear to be flYing … how we have to take off to show our true colors.

The cricket, with her muted-tone exoskeleton, displays her colors, a bright golden yellow only once she has taken to the air. As to the smallest of the flying folks, a hummingbird reveals delicate patterns of white, red, and black inside her lustrous dark green tail plumage only when she flutters around the feeder.

But … the greatest of wings are Nature's for her all-embracing masterY.

And then came Icarus, a true Pietà, in soft sandstone, perched on top of the hill. Icarus, the Greek hero who crashed into the sea. Icarus, the exuberant son who ignored his father's clear flYing lesson …

Steadying myself on two uneven rocks, I stand in front of the sculpture

I look:

The father holding his dead son becomes the mother of this Pietà

Placing myself under the skin of the stricken father
I feel broken

Icarus ignored his father's warning
to take the middle course.

I can't let myself be crushed under the burden of doubt and regret

I have to accept

I need to call on Mind, my main resource
My firmness of mind
My equanimity

EquanimitY, evenness of mind
The ... Way ... It ... Is ...

I believe in magic, I believe in the greatest *Yes* (Spirit) permeating Land, Life, Love ...

I have been curious about the maker of such a profoundly touching sculpture ... No signature. The only valuable piece of information is that it was done way before the place became a Buddhist center. What impresses me is the artist acted within the "forces of the unseen"—he could not have known that his creation, very much a typical Buddhist story, would end up in Buddhist territory.

The unbeknownst Greek "middle way," originates with Daedalus, the master craftsman, counseling his son. The father, designer and maker of the "aid wings," aware of the danger, advised his son to fly a middle course: "FlYing close to the burning sun will surely cause the waxed wings to melt ... or else, flYing close to the sea will wet the wings' feathery armature and weigh it down." The overly confident young Icarus did not listen to his elder's wise words and crashed down into what is now known as the Icarian Sea.

When you have eyes to see matched by a heart eager to listen, the opportunities for learning are infinite and never cease to surprise. It was unexpected indeed to realize that within nine days, filled with thirteen daily sitting and slow-walking meditations, I would end up flYing ... with the Daedalus/Icarus duo, along with crickets and hummingbirds as flying instructors. But then came along the porcupine disguised as a nonthreatening old hag. What did she have to do with flYing?

The apparition made such an impression that months later I dug deeper into the symbolism of the porcupine. I was amazed that the descriptions I found in my research ignored the fear associated with the protective quill armor; instead I learned that the porcupine is the symbol for "childlike innocence." It has "the power of faith and trust," while the other promotes the fact that "(it) seems to enjoy just about anything that it does. It has a strong sense of curiosity, and seems amazed and filled with wonder at most things it encounters." (From *Animal-Speak*, by Ted Andrews, and *Medicine Cards*, by Jamie Sands and David Carson, respectively.)

Now home, I let Nature's voices received during my retreat echo further.

The face that is in my heart stretches into a big smile. Spirit, the greatest *YES*, has sent me another song to help me answer the question, the quest that is guiding my life, "What Is the Spiritual in Art in Our Time?"

Life-As-Art is my answer, a beautiful seed that I (surprisingly) found within me once I lived a little. With more life, it grows into blossoms of childlike curiosity, wondrous awe, and luminous innocence. With my old hag porcupine messenger coming along to speak about innocence, freedom, and flYing, I am reminded of T. S. Eliot's poem "Four Quartets" as I realize "the end of all (my) exploring, (is) to arrive where (I) started and know the place for the first time."

Raising my arms in praise of the mYsterY, I become a *Y*, a *YES* spelled joY.

Come Closer

Jill Cooper

Come closer said the western dirt, the willing
ground, red, aware of its legends.
You may map me, but I want to know
you. Come closer. See the stratification
I carry in my satchel of time. See the red
and gold layers. It is the stratification
of your heart. It is a picture of the world.

Rest, here, in me, said the black basalt cavern,
there are no clocks here. Let your eyes
sink deep into the cool spaces
where everything that ever happened
happens again and again, reflected,
developed, and refined.

See the various worlds—the one of your
internal gaze, the one that ends only
with horizons and stars, the one of legends,
and the one world who knows herself,
and will teach you who you really are,
in this highest place, if
you will look.

Come closer, said the red earth.

A Study in Motion and Other Poems

Minna Aalto

A study in motion

Biking home under Clouds United scattering
I was once again introduced to the thought of all being one

(The interpretation of a point being made by nature is of course all
mine
But they did illustrate the probable state of affairs fairly clearly,
the rain and the sun and the half of the moon showing.
and the rainbow I missed but my sister saw,
all blending into that one moment)

Next thing I know is I'm writing a poem

Maybe to remember that one original thought just a little longer

again

A blessing for the day

dear fellow traveller, keep your eyes open for the love signs posted
all over,
and everywhere.
better yet, why not be a love sign yourself?

intimate knowledge

a friend of mine once told me that laughter
is the only sound which truly makes sense
i was starting to agree with her
already on my own
and now
all these days and nights
and the in-betweens with you
are convincing me
she was right

& dear love

Before doing the dishes
and before putting away the laundry
Before wiping away the crumbs,
and before pushing any more creations into being
through willpower alone

Before one more should, before one more must,
before one more if only, before one more one more:

Wait a While.

Your soul moves at the speed of light;
soon, you will have caught up with each other again.

Reason

Everything happens for a reason
might just be an optimist's interpretation of
everything happens

Well, reasons may be something for the mind to chew on,
yet I'm fairly sure my heart beats quite happily for none at all,
yes, even wildly at times

what i have inherited glows

as the outlines of my grandmother fade,
and as what she just recently still was translates into
memories
i slowly become sure, that rather than dimming the light
or turning away from the world
i am to celebrate.
what i have inherited glows.

Illustration by Minna Aalto

All Is Welcome Here

Verity Arndt

It's early, the sun has yet to greet the day; I rise and go to my special place. At first it seems as though all is silent, then gradually, with gentle attention to my own breath, the symphony resounds. Rain falls softly, sweetly, rhythmically. My heartbeat becomes strong and clear, its melody audible. This space-time is slow and easy. I am welcome. I am home. Here I say *Yes* to myself and to my experience.

All is welcome here. Every emotion that asks to be felt I feel. Without stories or words to the emotions, I simply feel. The sweet heartbreaking song of sadness that floods my heart, that asks to silently caress my face, my neck, my hands, and my heart, I feel. Yes. The unborn fear that hides anxiously in the cracks and caves comes in a flash to race across my heart, leaving me frozen and chilled. Yes. The powerful, dark, and dangerous anger that threatens like an all-consuming red star threatening implosion. Yes.

The hope that springs forth like a newborn flower turns its face toward the sun. Yes. The bliss that follows the pain, the dewdrops of grace, sparkling, fresh, unsurpassed beauty. A light that shines in every space in me. I am transformed into that light. Yes. All of these waves wash over me and I rise up through them and begin to surf each one. No emotion is feared or resisted and they all dissolve. I am fully here, fully present with it all, and all is well.

I see life from a grander perspective. I see clearly. Love pulses silently and powerfully. It's okay to be where I am, doing whatever I am doing. I can go anywhere from here. The worries that threaten to choke me, I don't fear. Just as I welcome the frustrations that swarm like gnats, I know that I can face whatever comes. I know this, because I am here for myself. I speak to myself as a loving and caring parent would speak to her precious child. I am soothed and comforted. I am in the soft presence of unconditional love.

All is welcome here. I can be like a child, light and carefree and dreaming. Oh, the softness, the uncontainable joy, the feeling of chasing moonbeams and flying on butterfly wings; the innocence and charm of seeing each new thing as if for the first time! Yes, my heart softens, yes. I can be a goddess, looking over her kingdom and confident in her power to transform worlds. I can revel in the deep inner knowing and maturity that comes with time; the fullness of vision, the power of adulthood, and the lush depth of a woman who knows exactly who she is and rides the waves of that knowing. Yes, my heart soars, yes.

I can be a dreamer, playing in the field of hidden dreams, in the secret places that are just for me. No one touches these dreams, they are mine and they can be boundless and whatever I wish. Every tear, every aching place, every bent head of despair, I transform simply by my presence. Yes, my heart sings, yes. I am the artist who creates landscapes that are so real I step right into them. I sing. I create sounds of honey with the gentle touch of my fingers on harp strings. Welcome, welcome, welcome. I let my imagination free! Yes, my heart thrills, yes! Yes to all the different aspects of myself.

All is welcome here in this judgment-free zone. There are no rules in this hazard-free zone. I can meditate or daydream. I can cry or laugh. I can fly. Breathing *Yes* into every experience, I am all that I have come forth to be in the world and I include all of life, every bit of it, and so life expands into the true fullness it was meant to be, in love.

In the heart of yes, I am free.

The Alchemy of Turning "No" into "Yes"

Donna Wetterstrand

I've always loved being human. So much so, from my teenage years on, I've kept an internal running list of the "Top Ten Reasons I'm Glad to Be Human." The list is Top Ten in name only, because I so often run across more—people, events, music, experiences, whatever—that clearly belong on my list.

So, saying yes to the human experience has been part of who I am since . . . forever. (When I was 11 years old, I won a province-wide essay contest on the topic "Come Alive." It fairly crackles with energy. I wrote about self-improvement and robbing banks. What were the judges thinking?!)

More deeply, in my precious time as a coach/counselor/mentor with the online enlightenment school Divine Openings, I've grown to understand that there are many ways of saying yes to life: It can look and feel like a huge leap into the unknown, or show up as a simple desire to feel just a little bit better. What better way to say yes to life than wanting to feel better? The daily small yeses can add up to feeling pretty darn good: the yes of a shared smile, the yes of kissing a child's cool cheek, the yes in a lover's eyes. Yes feels good.

The transformational direction yes takes us is always toward ourselves. One of the best tools for helping us say yes is the map of human emotions, our "instrument panel." You can use it to navigate the journey of your life by taking readings of your emotions: Where are you now and where do you want to be? Where were you yesterday? How far have you come? At the bottom we experience the heaviest, densest of emotions (rage, despair, fear) and, at the top, we feel the lightest, brightest of emotions (joy, bliss, spiritual ecstasy).

There's a truly magical spot on that instrument panel. To me it is almost alchemical in its mysterious power to shift "no" to "yes," and it shows up right in the middle of that range of emotions: it's called peaceful acceptance. Peaceful acceptance is the hero of human evolution, because it beautifully softens the resistance of "no" and then quietly, gradually transforms it to "yes," in a way that *sticks*.

Peaceful acceptance is a feeling that essentially says a quiet "yes" to whatever is happening in the moment. It takes the constriction of resistance and softens into a more open and allowing feeling. When resistance to what is happening disappears, our whole being can relax, and whatever we are experiencing will have the freedom to move and change, rather than getting stuck.

Accept your heartbreak. Accept your impatience, your rage, your jealousy, your despair. Accept that you don't have what you want. Accept your own foibles, and the shortcomings of others. Accept a sense of peaceful calm. Accept your transformation, too. Accept it all. Acceptance is the stuff miracles are made of.

Dwell Hard

Chelan Harkin

Dwell hard
on the theme
of "Yes"
tingle with it
on a regular basis
ask life,
"Can I get a light?"
Always and eventually
she will say yes.
If it takes time it's because
she has completely lost herself,
that Wild Woman!
in finding the perfect way
to deliver you
your own joy!
Be patient as she shuffles
through her limitless tool box
of form
soon, she will say a great big
"Aha!"
and rearrange all of existence
to open the universe
to you.

Meanwhile, move in
with your joy,
breakfast on bird song,
sunshine
and whatever makes the atoms
of your body
feel like confetti
and remind yourself
continually
of all the reasons
to be exquisitely
unworried
about everything

What?!

Chelan Harkin

Our atoms, pieces of arranged energy,
have come together
to make tools
out of us
so that we can sing?
Yes.
Really?!
Yes.
So that we can embrace
and feel each other's hearts
even though we are only
made of immensity
and brilliant, empty space?
Yes.
So that we can dance and know
Love
and have hands
made to serve
the One Great Heart
pieces of which
live within us all?
Yes.
Yes.
Yes.

Dreams Are Always True

Richard Grossinger

Once we concede that consciousness is based in something other than molecules and is self-authenticating, the whole universe opens up. After all, it's possible, quite possible, that if anything anywhere is conscious, then we are conscious, too, not only by syllogism but by superposition of all consciousness everywhere. What we are now is a temporary coalition or consortium of fragments, each of which can be independently whole, too.

We can turn into multiple beings, each of them us.

Pause for a moment and consider the ramifications of that.

Every day—in fact, every moment—we create our system anew.

We shine a pinpoint of identity brightly and exclusively on everything as we emanate from it. Yet we are not always skilled at moving that pinpoint into other pinpoints or views interdependent with us; we can't all of us seem to find the innate torque. If we could, just about everything on Earth that's broken would get fixed in less than a generation.

How do you get people to know that their thought-forms are convertible, endlessly convertible?

In truth, the facts explode from within, and almost always from directions in which we are not looking and in ways that we have forgotten or excluded.

Even a creature's absolute consciousness is not explicitly conscious of its entire multidimensional frame but, if consciousness has been inherent in the universe, before as well as after the Big Bang, then it is its own source (and destiny) and the source of its own mirage—any mirage by which it becomes known to itself, any self. Yes, we ravel and unravel in place.

Dreams are always true.

*

The above paragraphs have been excerpted from the unpublished fourth volume of the "Dark Pool of Light" series (North Atlantic Books), submitted by the author and arranged by the publisher (Exult Road). These excerpts form a "consortium of fragments, each of which can be independently whole too."

O Yes

Brian Doyle

Lately I have been delving into early Irish literature and language, and so have been raiding cattle in Cuailnge, and pondering the visions of Oenghus, and feasting at Bricriu, and wooing Etain, which last has led to some tension with my wife, who is of Belgian extraction and does not like to hear me tell of the beautiful Etain, the loveliest woman in all Ireland, although Etain was changed to an insect and banished for a thousand years, until she was reborn as the wife of Eochaid Airem, king of the green lands.

I try to explain to my wife that I am only wooing by proxy, as it were, and that Eochaid has the inside track, he being in the story and me only reading it. This line of talk leads me inevitably to Flann O'Brien and Myles na gCopaleen and Brian O'Nolan, all of whom I wheel into the conversation, the three men standing all in the same spot, as if they were the same man, which they were, except when O'Nolan was writing, which is when he became one of the others, depending on what he was writing (novels as O'Brien, journalism as na gCopaleen, which means "of the little horses"), or even others, as he apparently used a different name every time he took up the pen, which he did often, sometimes as Count O'Blather, or James Doe, or Brother Barrabus, or George Knowall.

My wife is unmoved; she will not have Etain in the house.

After a while I realize that the problem is the word *woo*. It is a word that may be applied to your wife and your wife only if you have a wife, she is saying without saying. She is a subtle woman, which is part of the reason I wooed her some years ago, and won her from various rivals, who did not woo so well, and went away, one may say, full of rue.

I spent some time after that saying *woo*, which is a very fine word, rife with meaning and emitted with a lift from the lips, like *whee* and *who*, or *no*. By chance I happened to be saying *woo* in the presence of my new son Joseph, a curious young man three months of age. Like his father he is intrigued by sounds, and soon enough he too was saying *woo*, and then my other new son Liam, also three months old, picked it up, and the three of us were wooing to beat the band, although then Liam burst into tears and had to be carried away to another room for milk.

Joe and I kept it up, though; he is an indefatigable fellow. After a while he switched to *who*, and I went with him, to see where this would go, and it went back and forth between us for a while, and then it went to *whee*, and then back to *woo*, and then my wife came back in the room and found us wooing like crazy men. By then it was Joe's turn for a suckle and off he went, and I went downstairs to raid cattle in Cuailnge, and ponder Oenghus, and feast at Bricriu, and woo Etain, of whom the less said the better.

The wooing of Etain demands a certain familiarity with the Gaelic tongue, which has fascinated me since I was a boy in my grandmother's lap listening to the swell and swing of Irish from her lips, which more often than you might expect had Gaelic oaths on them, as she was a shy woman with a sharp temper, though gentle as the night is long, and much mourned by many to this day. I still hear her voice on windy nights, banshee nights, saying to me, gently, *bi i do bhuachaill mhaith*, be a good boy, or *go mbeannai Dia thu*, God bless you. So partly in memory of my grandmother, a McCluskey before she was a Clancey giving her daughter to a Doyle, I have been marching through the thickets of the Irish tongue, the second oldest in Europe behind Basque, and the cold hard fact is that the Gaelic language is a most confusing creature, and although I don't understand very much of it, I read about it at every opportunity, and have been able to note several interesting observations on small scraps of paper, which are then distributed willy-nilly in various pants pockets, emerging here and there like crumpled fish, and reminding me that I had meant to write an essay on the topic at, or more accurately in, hand.

Thus this essay, which was supposed to be about the fact that there is no way to say the words *yes* and *no* in Gaelic, but which has swerved unaccountably into a disquisition about sounds, of which some are exuberant, like Joe's *woo*, and some affirmative, like *sa*, which is Gaelic for it is, and *yes* and *si* and *ja* and *oui*, which are English and Spanish and German and French for *yes*, which there is no way to say in Gaelic, try as you might.

Is it sayable in the Irish?

Nil—it is not.

Nil is as fascinating as *sa* to me, especially so lately because my daughter, a rebellious angel, age three, is fixated on *no*, which she says often, in different accents, with various degrees of vehemence. She says it morning, noon, and night, particularly at night, when she wakes up screaming *no no no no no*, and answers *nooooo* when I ask what is the matter. Sometimes she says *neuwh*, which is a sort of *no*, which is said usually after she has been watching Mary Poppins and is afflicted with a sort of stiffening of the upper lip which prevents proper *pronounciation* of simple words like *no*. It is interesting that she is riveted by *no*, because her brother Liam is riveted by *ho*, which is the only word he owns at the moment. Like a geyser he emits *ho!* regularly and then subsides. I expect him to pick up *no* pretty soon, his sister being a whiz at it and the boys certain to learn at her knee, and then Joe will get *no* too and then my children will be saying *no* to beat the band, not to mention the thin stretched rubber of their father's patience, which they hammer upon like a brittle drum.

But their father is in the basement at the moment musing over the fact that Gaelic is the only language on the Continent that always uses *tu*, or thou, when speaking to one person, or *sibh*, you, for more than one, which habit, he thinks, reflects a certain native friendliness in the tongue and in its speakers; and he further puzzles over the fact that Irish counts in twenties, not tens; and further he muses that Gaelic at least in Ireland has no terms for the *Mister* and *Señor* and *Herr* that English and Spanish and German use as terms of bourgeois respect, which makes him wonder about Irish independence as well as rural isolation. Also he spends a good deal of time pondering Ogham, the alphabet used in Ireland for writing on wood and stone before the year 500 or so, when Christianity and the Latin alphabet rode into Ireland together on strong winds, and the fact that Gaelic has perhaps 60 phonemes, which are sounds that convey meaning, and of which there are perhaps 44 in English, which comparative fact makes me wonder about the width of the respective languages, so to speak, which width is also reflected in the simple spelling and pronunciation of terms in each tongue: I might say of Liam that he is *an buachaill*, the boy, for example, and roll the Gaelic off my tongue like a song but pop the English out like a button, rather like *ho!* which is what Liam is saying as I am calling him *an buachaill*.

Further I am fascinated by the fact that Gaelic is a language in love with nouns, as can be seen with a phrase that often occurs to me when I think about my daughter's and my sons' futures, *ta eagla orm*, which in English would be "I fear" but in Gaelic is "fear is upon me," which it is, like a demon between my shoulders. To exorcise it I sometimes whistle; in English, "I whistle," just so, but in Gaelic *ligim fead*, I let a whistle, or *taim ag feadail*, I am at whistling.

I am at whistling a great deal these days, it turns out, trying to get the fear off me. For I am terrified of the fates that may befall my children—fates over which I have no power at all, not the slightest, other than keeping my little new people close to me in the presence of cars and dogs and such. So there are times now, I can honestly say, for I am sometimes an honest man, and admiring always of honesty, that I am exhausted by, and frightened for, my raft of children, and in the wee hours of the night when up with one or another of the small people I sometimes, to be honest, find myself wondering what it might have been like to not have so many.

It would have been lonely.

I know this.

I know it in my heart, my bones, in the chalky exhausted shiver of my soul. For there were many nights before my children came to me on magic wooden boats from seas unknown that I wished desperately for them, that I cried because they had not yet come; and now that they are here, I know I pay for them every minute with fear for their safety and horror at the prospect of losing them to disease and accidents and the harsh fingers of the Lord, who taketh whomever He wishes, at which time He alone appoints, and leaves huddled and broken the father and the mother, who begged for the joy of these round faces groping for milk in the dark.

So as I trudge upstairs to hold my daughter in my lap, and rub my old chapped hands across the thin sharp blades of her shoulders, and shuffle with sons on shoulders in the blue hours of the night, waiting patiently for them to belch like river barges, or hear Joe happily blowing bubbles of spit in his crib simply because he can do it and is pretty proud of himself about the whole thing, or hear Liam suddenly say *ho!* for no reason other than Liamly joy at the sound of his own voice like a bell in his head, I say *yes* to them, *yes yes yes*, and to exhaustion I say *yes*, and to the puzzling wonder of my wife's love I say *o yes*, and to horror and fear and jangled joys I say *yes*, to rich cheerful chaos that leads me sooner to the grave and happier along that muddy grave road I say *yes*, to my absolute surprise and with unbidden tears I say *yes yes O yes*.

Is this a mystery and a joy beyond my wisdom?

Sa—it is.

Part Five

Love

Yes

Fred LaMotte

. . . and his heart was going like mad and yes I said yes I will Yes.

—Molly Bloom, Ulysses

There are many faces, but only
one smile.
When love grins, worlds are born.
When the heart is quiet
the mind just keeps nodding and babbling
yes yes yes like Molly Bloom.
It's the kind of conversation
everyone should have
between the head and the heart,
one perfectly still, the other
perfectly mad. . . .
O friend, you never need
to silence your mind!
The path of craziness leads to the stars.
You never need to stop seeing otherness
just because all faces are yours.
I learned this from the one
who was given to me
as a Gift.

Molly Bloom's Yes Soliloquy

Patty McCabe-Remmell

Yes because he never did a thing like that before as ask to get his breakfast in bed with a couple of eggs...

Some of us, when we are on the edge of sleep, sink quickly and deeply, forgetting the cares of the world for abandonment to the subconscious machinations of the mind through dreaming. There are others of us, however, particularly after being awakened in the middle of our night's repose, whose minds unwind the tapes of the subconscious. We do not drop lightly off to sleep. We are thinkers: creators with so much data running through our conscious thoughts that our subconscious often has to wait, like an anxious assistant, to update and process. It is in these long stretches of wakefulness that we think the private things, the things we can't say out loud, the things that allow our egos room to stretch. This is when we can indulge the inner child that needs and wants, when we can parade naked before our inner mirrors, critical of ourselves, self-conscious even, yet begging for affirmation, validation, justification.

Readers of James Joyce's masterpiece novel, *Ulysses*, often compare the character Molly Bloom, wife of Leopold Bloom, to the archetypal earth mother. She is Penelope to Leopold's Odysseus, the wanderer who returns, ultimately, to his wife's side (albeit in disguise at first). Avid Joyce readers—as well as many scholars—will point out that Molly is the creation of a masculine mind, however, so the validity of her femininity can be called into question (and often is); but Joyce was an astute observer of women: he grew up with sisters, and women are notably prominent in his short stories that make up *Dubliners*, as well as in *A Portrait of the Artist as a Young Man*.

And then there are the understandable comparisons of Molly to Nora Barnacle, the woman who eventually became Mrs. Joyce.

The initial yes in Molly Bloom's soliloquy seems odd at first, as surprising as coming 'round the corner only to catch someone in mid-conversation, but it's just Molly, thinking to herself. The reader has to "hear" that she is a little surprised—not so much that her man has come home drunk at two in the morning accompanied by a drunken guest, but more at the audacity of his demands. If the reader senses a little pique in her tone it is no wonder, because now she is awake, propped on one elbow and allowing her thoughts to tumble out, unstopped by punctuation, while she lays awake, unable to fall quickly back to sleep, and on the verge of her menses, ruminating while Mr. Bloom snores, his back to her, his head to her feet.

This succession of "yes" moments throughout the final episode of *Ulysses* (the chapter sometimes referred to by scholars as "Penelope") is the stream-of-consciousness that Joyce imagined went on in a woman's head. It is, on its surface, a delightful surfeit of romantic, descriptive soliloquy. After the incessant maleness of the previous seventeen chapters ("episodes," as Joyce titled them), the reader returns with Leo Bloom to home and hearth, where Molly awaits in the same bed in which she had romped earlier that afternoon with her lover, Blazes Boylan.

We move from "yes" to "yes" eagerly, following the train of thought that often gets sidelined. We are privy to her yeses, affirmations of her life, her station, her gender. Molly's soliloquy is possibly the most titillating of all the chapters, and so we read the soliloquy vicariously as well as voraciously, sitting inside Molly's head and affirming her thoughts along with her, saying "yes, I've been there, I understand." She speaks of power: social power, sexual power, motherhood power, and she affirms and reaffirms, choosing to say yes, at times putting some things to rest, saying "yes, I have this one figured out, put it aside," and moving on to the next. We want to say yes with her, say yes when she affirms, "yes, I want," or "yes, I understand." We want to say yes to her frankness because she's so free about it. She can't be buttoned down. She rejects the status quo and wants to break out, to be able to act like a man but be treated as a woman. She wants an equal say and we say "yes, this will come in your lifetime," and she wants permission to honor her body, enjoy sex without procreation, and have a good hearty laugh and a night out once in a while, and so we say "yes" because we want those things, too. We think about these things but never give them voice for fear of ridicule or condemnation. So we say "yes, Molly, think what you want to think, affirm your beliefs, forgive yourself, allow yourself to say yes."

The quintessential "yes" moments, then—the almost orgasmic finish before the denouement—appear in the final lines, the yeses coming closer together, building in pace and tension, the culmination of which drifts off as Molly falls to sleep and we are left breathless, in awe of the power of her affirmations:

> . . . *yes and those handsome Moors all in white and turbans like kings asking you to sit down in their little bit of a shop and Ronda with the old windows of the posadas glancing eyes a lattice hid for her lover to kiss the iron and the wineshops half open at night and the castanets and the night we missed the boat at Algeciras the watchman going about serene with his lamp and O that awful deepdown torrent O and the sea the sea crimson sometimes like fire and the glorious sunsets and the figtrees in the Alameda gardens yes and all the queer little streets and pink and blue and yellow houses and the rosegardens and the jessamine and geraniums and cactuses and Gibraltar as a girl where I was a Flower of the mountain yes when I put the rose in my hair like the Andalusian girls used or shall I wear a red yes and how he kissed me under the Moorish wall and I thought well as well him as another and then I asked him with my eyes to ask again yes and then he asked me would I yes to say yes my mountain flower and first I put my arms around him yes and drew him down to me so he could feel my breasts all perfumed yes and his heart was going like mad and yes I said yes I will Yes.*

Only One Word

Bash Evans

They speak of three words, I speak only of one…

Is that not who we are?

Nothing makes sense without acceptance

But still I wish to learn more about you

I searched for connection without presence and found

no one

but myself

In finding myself, I found a key, the key to you

Then it said: You will understand

There is more behind this word than most know

It is all that we are and offer

It is the bridge and our decision

It is the path from my heart to yours

You may love without consent

but to share that bliss with another

we only need to say that one word…

Yes.

Yes Yes Yes

Brian Doyle

If in the beginning a boy cannot for the life of him find the tongue
With which to express his interest in a path of further conversation,
And the girl for reasons of her own, and excellent reasons they are,
Cannot find the semaphorics to encourage him a little but not a lot,
And smiles and glances being as we know endless tangled thickets,
And their friends, for good reason, harbor the most pressing desires
To not be involved in any way whatsoever, because of the previous
Blame and recrimination pattern as shown in former misadventures,
To wit *why did you not stop me when you should have* and etcetera,
Then inevitably there comes a momentous instant when one or both
Takes a flyer on the whole proposition. We don't applaud this much,
But isn't this the essence of the muddled existence of homo sapiens?
And isn't it a remarkably *capacious* metaphor, if you think about it?
Against all sense and logic, with every excuse not to, we take a leap,
And most of the time we end up sprawled and humiliated and sworn
Never under any circumstances whatsoever for whatever imaginable
Reason may arise to do *that* again but we do, as our friends slap their
Foreheads in dismay before they run and make exactly the same leap.
It's the craziest system there ever was. Sure, occasionally kids result,
But what fascinates me the most is the illogic of it. The very fact that
We so often do the very thing that our brains are shouting *do not do!*,
Doesn't that *thrill* you, even as you cover your eyes with both hands?
Me too. You hardly want to admit it, and so often it's all a pain train,
But deep down, for example, as your friend reaches for the telephone
To ask her out, and you are shouting *no no no,* you think *yes yes yes,*
Don't you? I thought so. But don't admit it—he'll never forgive you.

My Primal Yes

Hallie Bradley

Zillah, Washington, 1958

It was a typical noisy lunchtime in the cafeteria at middle school. The line of students along the wall was mixed with groups of older boys and the cluster of girls I stood with. My friends kept whispering to me, "Are you going to do it?" I didn't know. I wanted to but didn't know how to say it. My breathing shortened as the line inched along but the anticipation grew. The boys kept turning their heads around, the girls kept whispering. Finally, eye contact with the boy who'd talked to me on the playground. I nodded my head "yes."

I was one of the only girls who had boobs at that time. I was young, voluptuous, and boy-crazy. There'd already been one incident when I was alone at home. A boy had come over and lain on top of me over a blanket. I resisted further advances, but the word was out. I was easy.

When the really cute boy started paying attention to me, I was ready. We would see each other on the school grounds way out in left field up against the corner bank where the red-brown sumac grew, away from prying ears, but there were eyes watching our every move. My newfound notoriety was yielding not only attention from my girlfriends, but from the boys, too. We were the excitement. Mostly we just exchanged idle nonsensical talk, but one day he asked if he could meet me on Saturday at the local park. Then the recess bell rang. He ran one way to his buddies; I ran the other to my group. Once in the building, the girls were clustering around me in line waiting to hear what we talked about. I told them he asked me to meet him at the park. They all knew what that meant.

The week dragged on until finally reaching Saturday. I made up a lie that I was going to my girlfriend's. Freshly dressed in pedal pushers and a blouse for the warm spring day with a cool breeze, I was burning up with anticipation. The pool wasn't opened yet, so the park was empty. Walking past the massive warehouse buildings, I picked my way across the railroad tracks between the rail cars. Down the dusty path to the small parking lot by the pool, I stomped the dust off my shoes and began to scout for my friend. I spotted him way up at the other end of the park, sitting on a picnic table. I waved but there was no acknowledgment from him until I got closer, then he smiled and patted the table next to him. My heart leaped and I hopped up. We engaged in idle conversation, him casually rubbing my knee, me leaning into his arm, feeling warm and secure. Then he put his arm around my shoulders; my breath cut short as I looked into his beautiful Tab Hunter–blue eyes. My heart pounded; my head spun. Then he slid off the table, reached for my hand, and said, "Come on, let's go this way."

We walked toward the edge of the park where the grass ended and the dusty earth sloped down to the lower incline where no one went. He was sure-footed. I slid a bit but he steadied my hand as he led me down, down to a little ledge behind a tree where we sat in the dirt. I felt awkward, not sure what I was supposed to do, but the kissing part was easy. I loved kissing. Then the arms were around me pulling me closer, twisting my body into his, my breasts pressed against him. Oh, it was heaven. The lip kissing moved to neck kissing as I pushed my body to his. His hand roamed to my blouse buttons and I felt the air across my chest. My shirt fell open as he pushed it off my shoulder. I was breathing fast, panting, as he slipped his hand over my cotton bra, rubbing the bump pushing under the material. Still the lip kissing, the neck kissing, more frantic and then a hand slipped up and under the bra while the other hand fumbled for the hooks. In his desire, he abandoned the hooks and shoved the bra up just under my chin. He ravaged my breasts. My face was burning up, my body was pounding in places I was ashamed to think about. My head was thrown back, little moans coming up into my throat, and then I heard it. My name. Someone was yelling my name. He froze. We listened.

"It's my mom," I said blankly. He sat straight up looking right, then left, and without a word, he bolted. Sitting in the dirt, I felt the air around me change from warm to cool. My cheeks were on fire. I sat in the soft, smooth dirt, seeing the twisted and broken brush around me for the first time, deserted, alone, empty. The passion drained out of me as I ran my hands through my hair and wiped the perspiration from my forehead. In a rumpled daze, I rushed to reposition my bra and refasten the buttons on my blouse.

Her yells got louder as she edged closer and finally peered over. She saw me. "Get up here right now!" she hissed, "Who were you with? You lied to me. You're grounded."

I half-crawled up the dusty hill, dirt on my clothes, dirt on my hands, face smudged. The air blew stronger at the top of the bank, comforting the harsh feeling of being caught. I kept my head down as I pulled myself over the edge of the bank onto the grass. A disheveled mess, I stood on the edge of the cliff with my head down. I lifted my eyes to the fury in her face, those warm, fuzzy sensations hovering just below the surface of my clothes. I was bare, exposed, as if she could see right through me.

As we walked to the car I scanned the park for any sign of my friend, wondering if he'd talk to me again, thinking about how it had been just moments ago, wondering about the next time. My mother's voice faded into the background as secret images darted through my mind. The boy's hand holding mine. His warm kisses. The place on my neck. The yearning. It would be my dream to escape into again and again. My raw place, my primal yes.

The Only Word Spoken

Genise R. White

To be wrapped up in you
I am safe
you are safe
love finds us here
where yes is the only word spoken

A yes protects
come dance
in the shadows
come to me
where yes is the only word spoken

Feel the yes in my breath
I am safe
you are safe
our yes feels safe
when yes is the only word spoken

Come to me!
Come, lover
into the shadows,
close your eyes, say yes
our yes is the only word spoken

Minotaur of My Labyrinth

Joanne S. Bodin

You devour me inch by inch
your thick bull-tongue, your
clenched teeth throbbing
for my maidenhood
your opaque hollow eyes gaze
into mine, sienna
your body that of a man
viral, thrusting
can I satisfy you this time?
must I surrender before
I weave my golden thread
through our labyrinthine world?
I say "yes" to the minotaur

Plaster

Kip Silverman

Your smile makes me
want to chew
through plaster

Your laugh annoys me
I cannot hear it
often enough

I never cared for flowers
until you pressed pansies
into my palm
And explained how
they made you weep
and turned every answer

into a yes.

Dark Harvest

Joseph Millar

For Annie

You can come to me in the evening,
     with the fingers of former lovers
fastened in your hair and their ghost lips
     opening over your body,
They can be philosophers or musicians in long coats and
    colored shoes
and they can be smarter than I am,
     whispering to each other
        when they look at us.
You can come walking toward my window after dusk
     when I can't see past the lamplight in the glass,
when the chipped plates rattle on the counter
     and the cinders
dance on the cross-ties under the wheels of southbound
    freights.
Bring children if you want, and the long wounds of sisters
     branching away
        behind you toward the sea.
Bring your mother's tense distracted face
        and the shoulders of plane mechanics
slumped in the Naugahyde booths of the airport diner,
     waiting for you to bring their eggs.

I'll bring all the bottles of gin I drank by myself
     and my cracked mouth opened partway

as I slept in the back of my blue Impala
                        dreaming of spiders.
I won't forget the lines running deeply
        in the cheeks of the Polish landlady
who wouldn't let the cops upstairs,
           the missing ring finger of the machinist from Spenard
whose money I stole after he passed out to go downtown in a
    cab
and look for whores,
           or the trembling lower jaw of my son, watching me
back my motorcycle from his mother's driveway one last
    time,
           the ribbons and cone-shaped birthday hats
scattered on the lawn,
                 the rain coming down like broken glass.

We'll go out under the stars and sit together on the ground
           and there will be enough to eat for everybody.
They can sleep on my couches and rug,
                    and the next day
I'll go to work, stepping easily across the scaffolding, feeding
the cable gently into the new pipes on the roof,
                 and dreaming
like St. Francis of the still dark rocks
that disappear under the morning tide,
           only to climb back into the light,
sea-rimed, salt-blotched, their patched webs of algae
blazing with flies in the sun.

Are You Scared?

Kathy Trapp

"Are you scared?"

"Yes."

"Why?"

Seriously? You have to ask me that? If you knew how I feel ... how I have always felt about you, then you would understand. You don't get it, do you? I have never allowed myself to be so vulnerable. Never let the cards slip too far away from my vest. Never spoken with as much naked honesty. Never felt what I feel when I look at you.

You sit there; perfect in all of your faults. My perfect mess. You are scarred. You are beautiful. You make others believe they can hang their own star in the sky. You create beauty from rags and debris. You open your mouth and words flow out like shining, garnet wine, making me deliciously drunk, making my soul sing. My dreams grow in your grace; and you hold the harvesting sickle.

You are so fragile. Your body betrays you with a weakness that belies the strength of your character. You focus on others, on their well-being, on caretaking, on giving your love, all the while neglecting yourself and slowly dying. All I ask is that you allow me the honor of taking care of *you* now.

Which brings me to this: you are a complete pain in the ass. You are the single most stubborn person I have ever met. Oh my GOD. Can you ever give in? What would happen if you admitted you were wrong? Would you explode? Would a fairy die somewhere? Listen carefully, sweetie: you screw up sometimes. Not often. But there, I said it. You screw up.

You find joy in the mundane, beauty in imperfection, and knowledge in simplicity. You are the music that fills the dark corners of my mind, enticing me to follow the lyric of your song into the light. You laugh with such impulsive abandon that I cannot help but join you in whatever joke is dancing through your amazing mind.

Unless, of course, you are pissed off. Then? Watch. Out. Holy smokes, hell? Pshaw. Hell is a holiday compared to your warpath. You have a long fuse, but my God, the payload on the other end is decimating. I don't want to walk on eggshells around you, but can you blame me? I have been in that firing line.

To say Yes to you is to say Yes to everything I feel about you. Yes to vulnerability. Yes to hurt. Yes to potential betrayal. Yes to healing from wounds that left scars so deep they feel like a permanent part of my landscape. Yes to allowing myself to feel in a way that every fiber of my being fears danger.

Am I scared?

Yes.

Why?

"Because I love you."

L. H. to E. V. H.

Lisa Hoffman-Reyes, Ph.D.

Saturday Evening
[Postmark, August 8, 1891]

My darling Eliza! It is ten years today since we married hands and said *yes*, I do. And yet, how much longer than that have I loved you. We have soared through dimensions, skipped into lifetimes, spun across ages together. Your absence I cannot remember nor imagine. But in this incarnation, ten precious years ago, a symphony of light sang *yes, now, you may, in this presence*. And ever since, we are side by side, in body and conscience, in being and essence.

How thankful I am for the chasm that seemed to separate us before that day. How full and fortunate a wait; how well it worked to dissolve my fears. Without its sentient *yes*, could I have understood your silences as prolific, feather-light, and flowing with milk and honey? Would I believe you wouldn't tire of my lips always tracing your wrist and drawing the curve of your waist? Brave imagination has rendered us ever in accord, Eliza, and ever electric.

Dear One, I love our days, wreathing shoulders on propped-up cushions edged in velvet and golden threadwork. I read to you Shelley of "the everlasting universe of things" and you teach me of "all that dwells within the daedal earth." We record our kisses on parchment, and seal our breath with sacred waxes: "I do adore you more as I live to see more, and feel more" … "Ever your very own, my beloved."

Eliza! With you, I withhold nothing, deny nothing, surrender nothing, renounce nothing. I lose nothing by you, only reap and harvest and benefit to the core of my being. I build, raise, craft, and create, to thank the divine good for the beauty of you and the bounty of the world. And at the interim end of our endless lives, I will sound a rapturous *yes* to the heavens from our beds of wildflowers, under our blankets of stars, where together we curl and fold into the night.

Bless you ever and ever, beloved.

Let's

Ellen Bass

Let's take off our clothes and fool around.
We can roll all over
like dogs off-leash at Lighthouse Beach. Let's rummage
through each other's body
like a Fourth of July blowout sale, pawing through the orgy
of tweed and twill, silk and sequins swirling up in flurries.
The Buddha says don't argue until it's necessary.
Let's shuck oysters,
wash them down with dirty martinis,
the table littered with pearly shell. We can fill
the bathtub and pretend we're looking out
at sunset over Tomales Bay. Your breasts
are lanterns flickering on the water.
Your hips are still California's golden hills.
This morning I opened an e-mail from Texas
that said I'm going to hell and you don't really love me,
but if I repent, though my sins be scarlet,
they shall be as white as snow.
Darling, it's good to know we have options
but for now let's get triplet Chihuahuas,
carry them around in patent-leather purses.
Drag your guitar out from under the bed
and sing "Rose of My Heart" again.
I'll hunt in the garage for my zills and coin-covered bra
and do the three-quarter shimmy down the skinny hall.
Let's not think about our children, miles away,
doing things we'd rather not know.

Haven't we carved enough statues?
You remember the meadow I rented for you.
You wanted it sunny and edged with trees.
I paid the old woman a hundred dollars
so I could lay you down under the sky's blue marquee.
The longer we're together, the less I can tell you.
But hasn't it been a long day?
The President of Infinite Sadness is sorry
she ever ran for office. She imagined
she'd be like those brawny angels
who lower you into the tubs of warm mud at Calistoga.
But monkeys are gorging on peanut butter
so science can prove fat makes you fat,
and the workers who grow roses in Ecuador
are poisoned so we can say it with flowers.
Tomorrow we'll write letters. We'll try harder.
We'll turn down the thermostat and bicycle to work
and you'll swish plastic bags in a sink of soapy water
where they float like the jellyfish they're mistaken for.
But tonight let's bring Bessie back for an encore.
Don't you want a little sugar
in your beautiful bowl?
Let's make some rain, let's invent skin,
give me your glorious, gorgeous, generous thighs.
The ghost of my mother's in the basement doing laundry,
offering the damp clothes that extra little shake.
Wouldn't she be happy
to hear us nickering and neighing?
Wouldn't she be happy to know
death is feeding elsewhere tonight?
I'll dust your eyelids with cinnamon
and braid those old feathers into your hair.
Morning will find us asleep on the roof,
our faces blank as the new day, just the mockingbird
in the neighbor's tattered palm
whistling a tune that sounds a little like a Persian raga,
that twangy sitar, raising the sun.

Prayer

Ellen Bass

Once I wore a dress liquid as vodka.
My lover watched me ascend
from the subway
like I was an underground spring
breaking through.
I want to stop wanting to be wanted like that.
I'm tired of the song the rain sings in June,
the chorus of hope, the ravenous green,
the earth, her ornate crown of trees
spiking up from her loamy head.
There are things I wanted, like everyone.
But to this angel of wishes I've worshipped
so long, I ask now to admit
the world as it is.

Remembering Her

Jude Dippold

I remember
the smell of her,
yes,
all puppy
and coffee;
and the sound of her,
yes,
the sweet singing
of her skin,
flushed with moan;
and the next-morning her,
yes,
sitting cross-legged,
writing,
one breast exposed,
sheened
with the wisdom
that gathers
on the skin.

Yes.

Between a Yes and a Hard Place

Michelle Motoyoshi

Ben was one of those guys that every woman falls for. It wasn't only because he was head-turning hot (he made my gay boyfriend literally swoon). He had a charm that drew you in like the smell of cookies baking. Sweet. Tempting. Had to have some. When he unleashed that charm on you, you wanted to indulge and damn the consequences. But his charm had a ubiquity that always troubled me; everyone got a taste. I didn't want his charm if it wasn't meant for me, if it was nothing but a meaningless ploy for attention. But he persisted, and well, I do love cookies.

Things started slowly at first—just meeting for coffee and the occasional lunch. Over time, the conversations became more intimate, the meetings more frequent. Whenever we got together, we'd feel that magnetic closeness, that addictive energy that makes you want to ditch clothing and dive headlong into the sweaty pleasures of warm, naked flesh. I liked how he would smile helplessly, sometimes even get flustered, when he would see me. I liked how I could bombard him with questions, and he'd never tire of them. He was a challenge emotionally, but then so was I. It helped us grow somehow. It made me feel connected. Slowly, reluctantly, I realized I hadn't felt this way in years. Not only did I miss that feeling. I wanted it, bad.

Despite my want, I left my feelings caged inside my doubt. I was never certain how he felt about me, and his behavior did little to part the clouds. His actions always seemed a baffling brew of yeses and no's. Sometimes he'd be very open and attentive, sometimes painfully distant. Sometimes he'd be very eager to see me; sometimes he was hardly available at all. I didn't want to scare him away with my need. I didn't want to jeopardize the newborn friendship that had taken so much time and so much care to create. We persisted uncertainly in this strange flirtation, neither one of us seeking clarity from the other. Until that Christmas.

As a mutual gift of sorts, we decided to journey into the city together. Over one of our coffee dates, he crafted the plan. "We can have breakfast at my favorite diner, then stroll around Union Square. Oh, and I hope you don't mind if we take BART rather than drive. I know it's not as romantic, but I'm having car trouble," he said, a hopeful smile cautiously emerging on his face.

I didn't yet notice the smile. "Romantic?" I replied, with a rather sharp streak of confusion in my tone.

I finally noticed his smile as it retreated. "No, uh. I mean..." he stammered.

"BART is fine. I like riding BART to the city. It'll be fun," I offered, hoping I hadn't caused him to retreat any further.

"Good," he said. "How's Friday?"

"Romantic" haunted my thoughts every day until we met. I wanted to know what that little slip meant. Had the word come up because of me or was someone else on his mind? Did it reflect his feelings about our special outing? Did it relate to me at all? Or was it completely meaningless? Half of me wanted to believe it meant something, the other half was still held hostage by doubt. The standoff rendered me mute.

We met in front of the station and walked up to the platform together. I chose a secluded bench for us, well away from the other riders. I sat, and he sat, close enough that his body brushed teasingly against mine. Then he took my hand in his and squeezed it, leaning into me as he did. It felt like an answer.

A myriad of emotions welled up inside me, flooding my mind, blinding me to everything but the sensation of our clasped hands. I knew this was the moment. If I wanted him, now was the time to act. He had opened a door. Every cell in my body rallied to make a move. Every voice in my head said, "Go!" Except for a single lonely, persistent one.

My husband's.

*

Marriage is tough, much tougher than you imagine going in. After over a decade of togetherness, the passion that inextricably bound you in the early years inevitably morphs into something different. You can't predict what that something different will be. Sometimes it is a deeper, more stable caring for one another. Sometimes it's open hostility or ceaseless frustration. Sometimes it is a slow, subtle drift that leaves a cold, gaping distance between you—or, in a word, disconnection. Regardless of which something different you end up with, you got there through years of dealing with conflicts, working through misunderstandings, and weathering the unique collection of shit-storms life happens to blow your way. It isn't easy.

Often what we do to get us through is ride the rails of routine. You work at your job. You tend to your kids. You tend to your house. You eat. You sleep. Lather, rinse, repeat. Ad infinitum. And you stuff all the hurt and disconnection and niggling little questions into a jar and shove it way back on the deepest, darkest shelf in your soul to be dealt with "when you have time." No matter when that moment might be, it never happens to be now.

Then one day someone comes along, a tantalizing little treat of a man, and he starts to shake up that jar of stuff you thought you had cleverly hidden away, shakes it up so hard that you can't ignore it anymore. You realize you have to open that jar, and you have to take a cold, hard look at what's inside, or it'll crack open and spill its contents in a reckless mess that you have no hope of cleaning up.

*

"Romantic" echoed in my mind when I woke up in the morning. "Romantic" put me to bed at night. "Romantic" could fill up what was empty; it could make the glass full. *Romantic.* What did he mean?

I let myself imagine that it meant what I wanted it to mean. I imagined the dates we would go on. I imagined hanging out at his place. I imagined finally placing my lips upon his, our tongues tangling, our bodies writhing together becoming one. I drowned in the passion I felt. And it felt damn good.

"Mommy, can you help me with my homework?" my daughter called from upstairs. Her request ripped me from my reverie.

"Yes, of course." I sat down with her at her table, and we went through her math problem together. Fortunately, it was an easy one to solve. Still, she looked at me with her sweet, grateful smile that never failed to warm me through and through. Instead of running off to my next task, as I often did, for some reason, I stayed and let that warmth linger as long as it wanted. Strangely, suddenly, it offered up a question:

How would this change, how would she change, if I chose "romantic"?

Later, as I made dinner in our kitchen, as my husband came home when he said he would, as I sat watching TV with him, as we so easily talked about our days, as we put our daughter to bed, as I looked at our house—our home—the question reminded me: this would all change. The trust we had built, the respect that remained, our inside jokes, the comfort of knowing someone was there. Was I willing to let it all go? More important, was I willing to take all that away from them?

As my special Friday approached, a deceptively simple and profound realization began to settle into my consciousness. Perhaps my glass was half empty. But it was also half full.

*

When we are young, we tend to think there are straightforward answers. We bifurcate the world into right and wrong, black and white, yes or no. As you get older, you begin to realize that life is never that tidy, your feelings less so. Even if you are convinced a certain choice is right, you recognize something must be relinquished in making it. Saying "yes" to one thing means saying "no" to another. What makes the decision "right" isn't its inherent correctness or its (rarely ever) obvious morality, but the heart behind it. Why am I doing this? Whom will it hurt? Whom will it help? These aren't questions you can answer mindlessly or in haste. You have to let them move in and live with you a while, even though they can be rather unruly roommates. But if you sit with them patiently and attentively, they'll eventually help you see what you need to see. Yes, no; stay, go. Ultimately, what matters isn't the particular answer. It's what you do with it.

*

I sat with Ben on that bench, my hand in his, relishing that intoxicating closeness. Flooded with possibilities. Hearing that single lonely, persistent voice in my mind—the voice of love, of trust, of home—my husband's.

I let go of Ben's hand, let that possibility go with it.

Alone on the way home, I decided to pick up some chocolate ice cream for my husband and daughter. They love chocolate ice cream. And so do I.

Homecoming

Martha K. Grant

Forty-nine and a half years later she's come home
from the store with packages of photo album sleeves.

Archival quality seems necessary now to preserve
the pictures of their wedding ceremony

which she had to scour the house to find,
still in the original brown envelope they were delivered in,

still lying in the bottom of the now disintegrating box
that holds her Bride's Book, that thick white album

of mementos, shower invitations, guest and gift registries,
and a single black-and-white wedding portrait, glossy.

Coming home to this marriage, after wishing for too many years
to be elsewhere, anywhere. Even, sometimes, nowhere.

Agreeing finally—and preferring now—to be *here.*

The Edge

Shirley "Rodeo" Landis VanScoyk

Charles has been dead three years, soon, and all my knives are dull.

Even so, when Fred came to visit with his family, I bought a beautiful roast of beef—something I do not do very often. He trained as a butcher and he loved these big cuts of beef, slowly, barely cooked, with rosemary and garlic pushed in. I was sure he was not getting such things in Iraq, and that he would appreciate that I remembered his preference.

I even had a chat with the butcher at the grocery store when I was picking it out, something else I do not do often. I wanted the butcher to pick out a really pretty roast, something another butcher would like. These cinematic moments only ever roll out in my mind, so I don't know why I keep trying—black-and-white film clips clattered through the projector in my brain, calendar leaves flying—me, finally morphed into an odd mélange of Ma Kettle grasping a flag to her chest and Aunt Bea in an apron holding a pie, adoring family paying homage to my efforts, the local butcher presenting a huge hunk of flesh into a light from above and saying, "Your soldier will appreciate this, Ma'am!"

At least I was expecting this at Wegmans'—a cut above—but instead, the young man (who apparently does not share my rich mental catalog of iconic images) merely pointed to the second one down, a three-bone-in rib roast, and said, "That one looks good," and reached for the waxed paper.

My oven is broken, the heating element at the bottom blown out during a period of dank depression when I might have left it on all night or maybe for a day or two. Maybe a week. The oven that broke was not the oven I ever wanted: it was cheap, from the scratch-and-dent store, and was supposed to make do until we had the money for the kitchen renovation. That money was going to appear shortly after every other single thing in our lives was taken care of. All oven-type activities now take place in a stand-alone, plug-in roaster, which is pinch-hitting for the oven I never wanted, until I get the stove I deserve, and that is where I put the roast when I get home. But lately I have been thinking, Maybe not. Maybe I will have a kitchen but not a kitchen, because after the kids move into the addition, am I going to do any real baking? I hardly use the roaster. Maybe I don't want a fancy oven anymore.

Which makes me wonder if it is sad or happy that I may be giving up the idea of a dream kitchen, which was the fuel for terrible arguments and intense middle-of-the-night cravings, and the hook that I hung all my martyrdom and justifications on. If I never, ever get a six-thousand-dollar dual-fuel, self-cleaning convection oven, and a stove with a built-in griddle down the middle—and I make that decision on my own, based on practicality and present need—if I give up that dream, that tightly held desire, the lack of which was the reality of just how truly my needs and wants have been denied, who the heck am I?

And who am I having this argument with now?

Soon the roast is done, and I rest it for half an hour. I have heard that the single biggest mistake home cooks make is not resting their meat. You see, you get your roast chicken or leg of lamb or roast beef out of the oven, cover it all over with foil, and let it sit for half an hour before you cut. This way the juices stay in and don't run out all over your cutting board. I am a great, knowledgeable cook. I have created wonderful, memorable meals for multitudes of people in a terrible kitchen for thirty years. Lasagna, meringues, steamed shrimp and stir fry, roasts and pot roasts, jars of tomato sauce and jam, pickled green beans and red beet eggs, Thanksgiving turkeys and chicken and dumplings, lamb rolled in rosemary and pepper, chocolate cookies and lemon sponge cakes, homemade pasta, countless loaves of bread. The SOUP! The nameless mishmashes of leftovers that turned out to be delicious.

I have done all this, I realize, in a kitchen that has two cabinets whose lowest shelf is eighteen inches over my head, a sixty-year-old stainless steel sink, exactly three feet of counter space, no dishwasher, one half-inch to spare if you open the fridge and the oven at the same time, missing floor tiles, and exposed plumbing traces to the second floor the cat uses to chase mice. My kitchen counter had little flecks of gold sparkle in it when it was installed after World War II, which you can only see now if you move the canisters. Not to mention seven doorways and two windows. All of these conditions grist for resentment and seething, stewing discontent and the springboard for imaginative problem solving and voilà moments. For instance, if you don't have enough counter space, you get a cutting board that fits over your sink—that adds two feet. And one that fits over the top of your stove—when the stove is off, that is another two feet or so. If you don't have a dishwasher and company is coming before the dishes get done, put them in the oven until the next morning. In the winter, you can keep your extra groceries on the back porch—it's cold enough. If you keep the stuff under your sink organized in plastic tubs, it is really easy to get them out fast when the pipes freeze and burst.

And now, possessing the wherewithal to make all those headaches and compromises go away, I suddenly am not sure I care anymore. I can buy that stove, I can have all new cabinets, I can have anything I really want, the way I want it.

I pull the carving knife and fork out of the block to carve the rested meat. Instead of the elegant slice I am expecting, I end up sawing and mangling. The roast falls apart in delicious but ugly chunks. I am ashamed: Fred is watching me and I feel exposed and pathetic. The knives are all dull. I don't know where the steel is and I don't know how to use it. Charles used to stand in the kitchen and expertly flick the knives back and forth and listen to me bitch about how terrible the kitchen was. I would ask and ask for a decent stove, a new floor—hell, it would have been nice to have an actual ceiling. He never said yes. He used to say, "Stop cutting directly on the counter; you are going to ruin this knife." I would retort, "I can't hurt this crappy counter and I am going to get better knives!" And then we would sit down and eat a fine meal and later that night I would go to sleep, feeling sorry for myself and what I had to put up with. He honed the knives, and I sharpened my resentment for decades. And now I know it takes just three years for both to lose their edge.

The Pretty Place

Patricia Zylius

My husband named this spot the Pretty Place.
When the baby's cries got on my nerves,
he'd hoist the boy and say *Let's go.*

What was pretty wasn't where we stood
with our son in the stroller babbling back at jays.
It was the scene we looked at in the distance—
sun glinting on the bay, a curve of pelicans.

Here there was only rocky dirt and rattling weeds,
a few slabs of concrete. Even this he loved—
he'd race the stroller over ruts and gopher mounds,
skitter on two wheels around sharp turns,
raising dust and the baby's squeals.

The land's a park now, grubbiness lawned over.
This afternoon the ghost of that young family
drifts beside me, whispering,
nearly tangible against my skin.

He roared a zesty yes to all of life,
the man I married, then unmarried.
How did I fall out of love with such exuberance?
Now that he is dead, he's everywhere.

Part Six

Everyday Heroes

Ordinary Yes

Barbara Scott Emmett

And the ordinary moon

keeps shining

in an ordinary moon-

bright way.

And my ordinary life

keeps moving

through each ordinary night

and each day.

And those ordinary events

keep on happening

in that ordinary special

kind of way.

For my ordinary life

is extraordinary,

when I live it

in a moon-bright way.

Mother's Mane

Lois Colton

In this one you are holding me on your lap. I'm a little bald-headed baby in a collared dress and, as I'm the second child, you look relaxed now in your role of mother. We are outside and it is a summer day, maybe in Erie because both Grandma and little hunchbacked Great Aunt Treva are with us in the picture. I know how much you loved your Aunt Treva, and it shows.

Daddy is standing behind us and is wearing a brown fedora roguishly set forward on his brow. His face is animated as usual, and he looks as though he's just made a funny comment that had made everyone laugh. I can almost hear his Southern-accented voice coming to me through the years.

Treva is standing beside you, the knee baby. Already three, she wears one of those crisply ironed cotton dresses that you used to make for us. I look at her admiringly, though I'm barely half a year old and haven't yet seen how she would learn to twirl the baton, play the piano without looking at the music, or design 60s fashions in New York. Treva's strawberry golden curls form a radiant fluff over her sweet, somewhat tentative face. She is standing with one hand on her hip in a jaunty manner, but her face doesn't match that body language. It reveals something else, something latent that my arrival would give legs to.

But you, Mother, are beautiful, so beautiful, just like Daddy always said. "Isn't your mother beautiful?" I remember him asking. "Whroot, Whroo!" he'd whistle when you came out dressed to kill in that silver polished cotton dress you made for dress-up. The one that had a wide boat-neck collar and showed off your square shoulders when your hair was wound up into a bun at the nape of your neck.

In this picture you are only 25 or 26, but the strength of your self-confidence shines through your eyes and smile. Maybe you just finished saying, "Oh, George!" to Daddy in response to his cleverness.

Grandma, rather full-breasted, dressed in a tailored suit and low-fitting hat, looks just like older women were so often depicted in the 40s movies I used to love. You appear to be ignoring the imposing presence of your mother to keep the peace on this bright day. I remember that often you did not.

Now, we all love having these sharp black-and-white photographs that Grandma took with her expanding Kodak. That was the camera she used to photograph models she was painting, but when she'd take our picture, we would each be carefully set in place and would then have to stay put while the camera's wonderful lens slowly did its work. During these photo sessions, wiggly me would often end up in tears after one of Grandma's sharp scoldings to "Hold Still!" No wonder so many pioneer families look strained and severe in those photos taken by an itinerant photographer with his glass plates.

But you, Mother, have learned to say yes to this process since, as the only child of an artist, you'd been painted and photographed by Grandma your whole life. Last summer when we four children divided more than 300 of Grandma's wonderful paintings between us, we laughed because Treva ended up with so many paintings of you—baby Mom sleeping nude in the Tucson heat, a pastel of 5-year-old Mom's Shirley Temple ringlets, teen Mom staged wearing a floor-length gown spread out around her, a bust sketch of Pomona College Mom, Treva—who at times still struggles with the fractious relationship between you that I see in her 3-year-old expression—picked her own gallery of Mom paintings.

But, Mother, the thing I feel like I'm writing around, even though it is so central to me as I look at this family tableau, is your hair. Your thick, chestnut waves pulled back from the round face and framing your snappy blue eyes. Your beautiful, beautiful hair draws me into this photo and is somehow so pivotal to how I see you, even now when, at 92, your hair has turned white and lost volumes. Your glorious hair set you apart, made you *my* mother, and filled me with pride and belonging. How odd, and how strangely intimate. And as I look at this picture and feel this attachment to you through my love of your hair, I hear my own son's words when he framed how much he missed me during his foreign-exchange year in Argentina by reveal-ing, "I felt such longing when I remembered your hair."

Grandma

Janet E. Ward

Dear Grandma,

In this photo, you are just as I remember you. Your hair in place, you exhibit complete calm with a quiet look and smile. Grandma, how did you manage? How did you do it?

When my "first" grandma died in 1921, Grandpa wrote to you in Norway that he had nine motherless Norske children to raise and he needed your help. Grandma, you owned a teahouse on Harstadt's harbor. I have walked the street where it must have been. But you sold your teashop, got on a ship, came to New York, rode the train to Tacoma, Washington, and spoke no English. Mom was tiny, but she remembered your coming, your kind eyes, your calm demeanor, and your smile. How did you manage?

Grandpa was so proud to have American children, he refused to talk Norske with them; instead, he worked to perfect his English. None of the nine children spoke Norske, not even the ones who were born in Norway. Grandma! How did you do it? Cooking for eleven people, *Boom! Powie!*

Mom told me that as you learned English, you had all of the children learning Norske. What a gift you gave them, teaching all that you knew about their proud Norwegian heritage.

How often people try hard to acclimate to a new land, trying to merge into a new culture and society, then lose all of their prior culture for the new. Not so in the Olsen family. You made sure of that.

Grandma, our family was so blessed by your coming; you showered the children with love. You taught them so much. I'm sorry I never told you how special you were to me. Your brother, Uncle Andrew, as a ship captain, brought many treasures from around the world as gifts. But you! You were the greatest gift of all to our family. Thank you for saying "Yes." Thank you for coming.

Your loving granddaughter

Lena and Her Mother

Alice Lee

Fatigue. Forgetfulness.
Crying all the time.

Lena doesn't
understand this
new old woman.

She doesn't accept her mother
this way.

She is angry and confused, most of all, sad.

Life isn't supposed to be this way.
It should be all right, good, easy.

What to make of this dependent, helpless, feeble woman?
How to fit her in that perfect life she supposes she once had?

Lena's younger sister, Kirsten, is a psychiatrist.
She thinks their mother' s depressed,
wants to start her on antidepressants.

I want to ask her mother about her life.
I know so little of it.

She's been a widow for more than forty years.
The husband fell down basement steps
carrying a load of firewood,
It was Christmas Eve.
Lena was 11, Kirsten just five.

The mother raised two lovely daughters on her own,
managing a flower shop too.
The village knew her well;
she arranged the funeral wreaths for the newly dead.

I am a flower, you say.
Yes, you are a rose,
a deep red rose, Mrs. Andersson.

And, like a flower, all things alive
will wilt and then die.
It's all part of the plan.

You, Lena's only parent,
are afraid to let go of this life.

Don't be afraid of the darkness.

Love life, Mrs. Andersson.
Love each day like a rose.

Fiddler of Spoons

Maria Kute

Thirty-three years ago, Tracy came to live with my family. I was less than a year old; he was nineteen. He was tiny, well under 5' tall and only 70 pounds, with dozens of half-moon scars on his perpetually tan hands and forearms, where either he had pinched himself out of boredom or other inmates of "the institution" had done so for him. Tracy was hunched over, hated to walk, and had been pronounced severely mentally disabled.

Above his bed in the institution, a sign warned, "Keep away. Dangerous to others." They needn't have worried; there was no risk of visitors.

When I was finally old enough to understand that one doesn't usually inherit nineteen-year-old brothers from "The Council for Retarded Citizens," I asked my family why they decided to make Tracy a part of our family. My parents simply said that they wanted me to have a brother.

And they were right. My brother offered me many joys and lessons beyond their comprehension. While in a baby walker, I discovered that approaching him in his rocking chair meant that I would get kicked quickly across the floor, blithely squealing, my walker's wheels rustling over the carpet. His frustration with this game once sent me bouncing down the basement stairs, screaming with laughter.

He never really hurt me, though, aside from a few pinches brought when compromisingly frustrated; he would get a perfect quarter-inch of flesh and twist. Through Tracy, I learned how to recognize and respect the space of anyone who was vexed, even if I didn't understand why.

My brother was the master of one-liners. St. Edward's church, where I found myself eager to shout St. Francis of Assisi's "Canticle of the Sun" every Sunday, was the birthplace of Tracy's voice as well. As Tracy wriggled about one Sunday in our old, stark wooden pews, Father welcomed us as a parish, inviting us to stand with: "Let us pray." Tracy had no high opinion of prayer, as it involved sitting down, sitting still, and remaining quiet. With unusual clarity, Tracy shouted into the momentous silence just before our flock's response: "Get the hell out of here!"

Thankfully, not all of the lessons I learned from Tracy involved the threat of excommunication or head trauma.

He encouraged me to ignore people who would be bitter at my or anyone else's happiness, as when we came into restaurants and Tracy's distinctive shriek of joy echoed out. His hand, cramped with excitement through his middle, ring, and pinky fingers, covered his mouth in a claw of glee. Certain families would cringe, slicing their eyes diagonally at us through shaded lids. We, however, were too busy cutting up, relishing the joy of my youngest oldest brother.

Other people would begin to laugh, deep-seated belly laughs, when they heard Tracy and realized that this sudden explosion of unbridled happiness came from little more than a Mountain Dew or a "hee," as he called tea. "Hee" was his favorite word, as told by the volume at which he said it and the excited round of "AHHHH!"s that followed.

Tracy dazzled any room with his laughter and screaming. It pealed and reverberated over almost any restaurant and any family member's house where we were gathered to eat, especially "Ho ho's"—as Tracy called our grandfather. Years later, we finally realized that Tracy was just responding in kind to Papaw's standard greeting: "Ho, Tracy!"

Ho-ho's house always had the biggest spread of Kentucky delights: buttered rolls, green beans from his garden, and Mamaw's fried apple pies, to name just a few. Tracy would take breaks from eating only for deep gasps of air, as if he had gotten so carried away with the food that he forgot to breathe. This, of course, led to many *musical* exploits, as we politely named them, while my family would try to get him to expel the extra air by lying stomach-down on the floor.

Years later as a voice student, I learned the musical potential inherent in Tracy's talents. A beloved teacher referred to singing as "controlled screaming," emphasizing that I had to learn to make my diaphragm work by engorging myself with breath. I envied my brother's breezy aptitude and elastic stomach!

Because of Tracy's ability to retain air in his abdomen so well, he also became notorious for his ability to float in deep water. He made swimming a spectacle, as he stood in ten feet of water, arms outstretched in a "T." People swam around and underneath him incredulously while he remained motionless from the shoulders down with a balance that any gymnast or yogi would envy. Tracy chortled and screamed with delight as he splashed the water with his hands, still easily floating from his natural gaseous life balloon.

For the opulent exuberance Tracy shared with us, the ways we could help him seemed so small in comparison. When his legs became chapped he would walk toward us with the gait of an egret, Eucerin bottle in hand. "Do you want some lotion, Tracy?" "Ocean," he would reply. Other times, when he looked sad or frustrated, I asked him if he wanted a kiss. Every once in a while, my peck on the cheek could make him say "AHHHHHH!" with almost as much joy as "Hee!"

Less than two years after my father passed away, Tracy's abdomen began to swell, this time without relief. He could not tell us why or where he was hurting, and liver cancer claimed him at the tender age of forty-four.

While I was flying to Louisville to see my dying brother, it occurred to me that everyone should have a brother like Tracy, but almost no one did. Rather than grief, gratitude overtook me, and became a creature modeled after Tracy himself, stretching sinewy tanned limbs toward the sun. Miles above the earth, I wept. Unlike the deafening quiet I faced in the wake of my father's death, Tracy's rhythms propelled me into a fete of thanksgiving. I jotted down "Jo-jo," the evil imaginary friend who got Tracy in trouble. We blamed Jo-jo when Tracy was frustrated enough to cry or pinch anyone in sight, including himself.

While he swung on his swing set, he would sing "'et'cher hand down, woe-woe! It yer hand down, woe woe!" His incantations seemed to guard against anything that could cause regret. Now the beneficiary of Tracy's presence on earth, how could I be sorrowful in the face of a life with absolutely no regrets? Ten years later, I marvel at the wonder and music that permeated Tracy's life. I am still too grateful to grieve with tears of anything other than exultation.

My family would often communicate in singsong with Tracy, and together we would say in tones what we could not say in words. I no longer sing the "Canticle of the Sun" on Sundays, but the song of my father to Tracy plays in rounds constantly on my lips: "Tracy Lynn McJones is my beau, he's my gum-boy-ee, and his heart is golden cause his family loves him all the time." I don't know if paradise awaits true believers, but I know that to Tracy, it was no matter. He made his paradise here.

It is Tracy's buoyancy, tenderness, and playfulness that I will attempt to carry on with me. I say " Yes! Hallelujah!" to the blessing of Tracy, the kisser of ladies' hands, the fiddler of spoons, the lover of water and helium balloons. I will follow Tracy's lead, stretching my limbs to the sun, rounding my belly in swells of praise. Perhaps then, I can truly yell "Get the hell out of here!" when I feel stuck, and feel no shame when I exclaim in ecstasy to the world that I have "HEE!"

I will forever hold him in song as my golden-hearted gum-boy-ee.

Caught in the Rain

Kay Schmerber

On that long ago afternoon, standing on the sidewalk, she turned to wave goodbye to Auntie standing on her front porch. "Don't get caught in the rain," Auntie warned just as the heavy wet drops slid from her short bangs to her nose. As she trailed a few steps behind her older sister, she began to worry about how the rain knew what she did, and what it could do to her if it caught her. Wasn't rain just a little bit of friendly wet until it became a lot of wet, filling boots like buckets or boats? Rain didn't ever seem to care what she did or thought. That was the fun of rain. Before that afternoon, she could just wonder what doing this or that, or thinking that or this, would feel like inside herself. Now, the rain could catch her.

Years later, while skinny-dipping in a lake on a clear moonlit night, she recalled the teasing tickle of rain between the threads of her hair on that afternoon long ago. She imagined what it would feel like inside to stand naked in a light rain or soaking downpour. Wondering about this and that again, she began to invent rain in green, secluded places: deep backyard lawns, or forest hillsides beside old logging roads. There would be a wide night sky, and no neighbors nearby; no cowering "nay, not today" or pragmatic whispers that say, "Why don't you just take a shower?"

Standing at the kitchen sink late one night after dinner, her reflection transposed on tiny drops chasing each other down the pane, she recalled her ancient rainy wonderings and how they felt inside. The drumming on the roof grew louder. She dried her hands carefully, stepped out of her slippers and sweatpants, and skinned her wool socks down into a heap at her swollen feet. Tugging her arms free of her tight sleeves, she paused only to turn off the kitchen lamp.

The old back porch planks were already slippery. Harsh gravel gave way to glassy cool grass. Turning her bare feet slowly, her arms rose. Her chin touched the sky. There was nothing left to arrest the raw flesh of this thirst. Rain filled her throat, fell like tears, and caught her inside out in naked delight.

The rain wondered what took her so long.

Seaside Heartsong

Heather Sisson

Yes, new places.
Yes, new beginnings.

Songs and longings blur together into background music.

She tips her head, appraises
the weathered wood of the porch,
the indigo door,
the aged swing to the left, asking for another coat of paint,
the soothing bank of sea sprayed windows studying the water.

The flower garden reclines, snuggling the cottage
foundation waiting
for the push of pleasant weather
to pop into a colorful apron,
its strings a lengthy hug reassuring someone on a bad day.

Yes, it needs work—
some things worth having do.

She unlocks the rickety screen door sentry to find ghosts,
furniture playing dress up in linens, varying degrees of white.

High shuttered windows permit passage of sunlight's
faintest rays.
Rays exaggerated when
dancing with dust particles, mingling in swirls.

Grownups can't run away?
Got to be dependable?
And responsible?
And practical?

Others don't understand - they can't.
They can't.

She shakes her head, erasing the unwanted memories.
Her shoulders relax down, her chin rises up.

Her lips whisper, "Yes. This is mine, all mine."

Twirling with arms out, her faded flowered skirt expands,
the silent base of a hand bell in this reclaimed church.
This home forgives.

Spinning more dust up to dance she finds herself.
Happy again.
Head dizzy.
Heart centered.

Part Seven

Children and Wonder

The Temporary Body

Heather S. Friedman Rivera, R.N., J.D., Ph.D.

I had no intention of being a past-life researcher. In fact, if someone had told me I would one day become the founder of a research institute, I would have laughed myself silly. Yet here I am conducting scientific research, publishing works about past lives, speaking about past-life regressions, and hosting annual retreats. How did I get to this place? It still boggles my mind.

As a Registered Nurse, I was content to work and live in the world that I could see and that could be measured—until 1997, when I was diagnosed with rheumatoid arthritis. For the first time, I became restless and unfulfilled. Western medicine, no matter how helpful, could not heal me. I ventured outside my comfort zone and read about unconventional, alternative, and complementary therapies. I learned about acupuncture, biofeedback, channeling, and hypnosis.

Hypnosis and past-life therapy were not areas with which I was familiar or comfortable, but I was intrigued. I called a local hypnotherapist, Dr. Donna Kannard, who specializes in past-life regression therapy and made an appointment. I was curious and up for an afternoon of entertainment. I told the therapist nothing of my search for better health. I also warned her that I was a skeptical, nervous, and tense individual who probably couldn't be hypnotized. She listened to my concerns without judgment and in a soothing tone invited me to sit back in the chair.

Dr. Kannard guided me into a relaxed and peaceful state. Next she had me descend an imaginary stairway into a garden, wherein I came upon a library. I entered. There was an entire section of books with my name on the binding. I pulled one out and sat at a table. As I turned the pages, one page called to me. It was a drawing of a knight with a white horse kneeling before him. Before I could take another breath, I was pulled into the knight's body.

I was startled that not only was I able to be hypnotized but that I was now experiencing this knight's life as if it were my own. I felt the heaviness of armor, the hunger in my belly, and a soldier's sense of duty. I was able to hold two thoughts in my head simultaneously—those of the knight and those belonging to me in my current lifetime.

Suddenly I found myself dying on a battlefield of green, looking at the gray sky, stabbed in the throat during a battle. As I choked and gagged on blood, I was also choking and gagging in the therapist's chair. Despite Dr. Kannard's instructions to detach and watch the scene as if observing a movie, I chose to stay with the knight and experience his death. He took his last breath and I left the body, rising higher, becoming huge. In this space out of the body, I felt an overwhelming sense of love and peace, connectedness with all, and a sense of expansive oneness. I could have stayed forever in this way.

Back in my present-day body, I acknowledged that I had a direct spiritual experience and had experienced profound physical healing. I had suffered from chronic laryngitis for many years, and this past-life experience restored my voice permanently. Did remembering being stabbed in the throat in a past life resolve my vocal issues in my current life? At first I wondered if it was a coincidence or a fluke, but as the days, weeks, and months went by, I realized that something dramatic had happened to me. Before the past-life memory, I spent most days speaking at a whisper. But after reliving my life and death of the knight, I spoke with a clear, strong voice.

Not only did I have a physical healing but I had my first direct spiritual experience. I realized that I am not only Heather. I'm not only the knight, either, or any of the other past lives I've remembered since that first experience. I am an awareness currently inhabiting the temporary body of Heather. Since my out-of-body experience, I have come to realize that I said yes to this current body for my greater good. My purpose is to live fully in Heather's body. That means allowing myself to be everything I am. While in this body, I embrace life as Heather .

Deeply changed, I took a couple of days off work to process this restructuring of everything I thought I knew. Something had shifted inside my heart and mind. I was healed, and I felt an intellectual and emotional resolution in my core; I decided to live from a center of authenticity from that day on.

Since that first experience as a knight, I have devoted my energies to researching past-life therapy and writing about it. My books, *Healing the Present from the Past* and *Quiet Water*, were born from my new understanding. I founded a past-life research institute and continue to speak on past-life regression therapy. Saying yes to mystery, to authenticity, and to my own experiences has brought healing, comfort, and a life of great joy.

I Say Yes to Wonders

Mariann Martland

I say Yes to the burning heat of the fiery sun
To its promise to set
And its vow to rise

I say Yes to the tidal pull of the moon
Making me drown in my mind
I say Yes to breaking

Falling into the cold pool
and allowing the ache. I say Yes
Feeling every good, bad, or indifference

The world has to offer
I say Yes to truth
Feeling every inch of its beating heart

I say Yes to silence
Letting go of its captivating forces
Letting in its restorative powers

I say Yes to the wonders
To the ever-changing forces that sprout doubt and faith
To the uncertainties that bury my soul in darkness

To my beautifully scarred and flawless, ugly self
As I lift my eyes up to marvel in the mystery of the light
I say Yes to living
I say Yes to wonders

Chicken with Feathers!

Ille C. Gebeshuber, Ph.D.

Yes, it is a magic place. The virgin rainforest! Malaysia is a modern, hot, and humid country in Southeast Asia. Lots of high-rise buildings, asphalt on the streets, no sidewalks, no bicycle tracks, everything optimized for car traffic. Many people spend their lives between air-conditioned apartments, air-conditioned offices, air-conditioned cars, and air-conditioned shopping malls. So did I, for the first few months that I lived in Malaysia. I got fed up with this routine pretty fast. I wondered, "Is there anything else to do here apart from shopping, eating, and watching movies?"

I started to ask around and I finally met a woman who said, "Yes, there is. The Malaysian Nature Society. Join them; go on trips with them; get to know the beauty of our natural habitats." Perfect! I signed up for my first trip. Borneo. Magic Borneo. I cried when we landed on the island of my dreams. With four-wheel-drive cars we left the city of Sandakan, already weird and strange and different, heading toward the Danum Valley conservation area.

What I realized first when entering the forest, and what still causes me a lot of joy whenever it happens, especially when the transition is fast, is the change in temperature. Outside, on the streets, it is hot. Unbearably hot—hard to walk, impossible to ride a bicycle. But as soon as I step into the forest, it is cool. Good, nice, fresh air. And the sounds—all different. And the sights. The eye calms down. The heart calms down. The soul starts to fly. In this cool, shaded, tranquil environment, everything suddenly starts to make sense. It all belongs together, it all plays together, it all acts together, all organisms depend and rely on each other and grow together.

Nobody and nothing is useless. Even in death, all creatures serve as food or fertilizer for the others. No major destruction, no money, no rich and poor. What we have instead are circular processes, the perfect realization of the waste-to-wealth concept, local harvesting, sparse usage of metals, and no usage of plastics. The organisms in the rainforest: They grow, they thrive, they all live in their own time, and they are so beautiful. So beautiful. Life in the virgin rainforests still thrives in all its diversity, abundance, joy, and silence. And loudness! Sleeping in a hammock outside, waking up in the middle of the night to the sounds of Borneo pygmy elephants playing on the riverbank—oh yes, I felt that I am a chapter in the amazing living book of life itself, with all its grandeur.

I feel at home as soon as I enter the forest. And I can transfer this to friends, students, and colleagues. I begin to conduct biomimetic jungle walks with kids and grownups, too. But they can't all come to countries where rainforests exist—such as Thailand, India, New Zealand, or Malaysia.

"So you are doing virtual jungle expeditions in countries where no rainforests exist? How about in my country, Austria?"

Yes, it is possible to go on a virtual rainforest expedition in Austria! The kids are excited: "Ahh, we have to walk in a line. Ah, the one in front has to look back frequently to check if the one after him or her is still visible. If not, we just wait. If everybody does this, the group stays together, even without words." Groups in dangerous habitats do it like this all over the world, the Austrian kids learn from Oliver Futterknecht, my Austrian physics engineering student.

Oliver loves the forest, just as I do. Oliver is good with kids. We leave the Steyr University of Applied Sciences, where we just gave a talk on Malaysia, its animals, and what we can learn from the forest, and we jump on the bus that brings us to the island on the river in the Steyrer Au, Upper Austria. We are a group of fifteen kids between nine and eleven years old, three young adults in their twenties, Oliver, and myself.

"So, although far away from tropical rainforest, kids find a lot of inspiration in semi-wild places?"

Yes! The Steyrer Au is not the jungle. It is a place in the middle of civilization, and it smells like dog shit. I hesitate for a moment, and think, Was this a good idea? But then, living Nature captures us.

We play with plants, with seed capsules that explode when we touch them. We enter the forest and find blue wood. We see snails, with tiny high houses, and I tell the kids how amazing it is that the snails make their minerals, their crystals, at ambient conditions, without heat, without mining, just by local harvesting.

We see a spider and its web. First, the kids are afraid. Ah, a spider. I tell them how they weave their web, which kind of smart backup systems they have in the thread so that it does not break even if a huge insect flies in. I tell them about the golden spider in Madagascar, whose web is so strong that it stops bicycle riders. We find many different empty snail shells. We see rotting leaves, and how mushrooms grow out of the leaves—new life being fed by dead plant material. A girl finds an amber necklace!

We hug trees; we look at the veins of leaves. With amazement, we admire climbing plants that use large trees to climb up toward the sun. We smell soil and talk about slime molds. We touch feathers, realizing how much more sensitive the lips are than the fingers. We think how impressive it is that plants "eat" the gas we exhale and we breathe what plants exhale. We lie on the floor, watching ants communicating with their antennae, and we think about their invisible communication via scents so sublime and different that we cannot smell them. We climb up trees. We collect beauties (but do not harm anything that is alive) and store them in the containers each of us wears for later scientific examination in the lab.

"You mean, time was flying and the impressions were deep and far-reaching?"

Yes! Too soon, the two hours in the forest are over. The world on these 500 meters hasn't changed very much during the last hours, since we left for our virtual jungle expedition, but our perception has changed—and, with it, everything! And this is what's important. We head back to the university, where the microscopes wait for us to examine at high resolution what we collected.

Ah, this is wonderful. They reconnected with Nature. And so fast! I realize, especially in the kids in the city, withdrawal symptoms from Nature that concern me. Last time in Singapore, when we went to see a farm, the kids were pointing at the flock, exclaiming "Chicken with feathers! Chicken with feathers!" For the first time in their lives, they had seen chicken with feathers. They are only used to the blood-less, featherless, faceless whole chicken in the supermarkets.

Yes! Children need time in nature. Not only is it informative; it makes them happy. Just take them on a walk, outside to the wild, just a tiny little wild spot, even in the city will do, and let them smell, listen, touch, taste, feel, hear, see. The "jungle" is everywhere. And respect for the real thing starts by appreciating the small. No need to rush through life. No need. Enjoy and do good!

*

If you want to hear more on this and other things we can learn from living Nature, listen to Prof. Ille's TEDx talk "What Is a Physicist Doing in the Jungle?: Biomimetics of the Rainforest" on YouTube.

Yes!

Leela Rain Eberhardt, age 4

Yes is my favorite word.
Yes means you can have it.
Yes means you can want it and you can have it.

Yes means you can have a little piece of candy after dinner.
Yes means you can have a hamburger like Ms. Sheila's with the
little buns.

Yes means if you want a jacket, you can have a jacket if you're cold.
Yes means you can go play in the rain.

Yes means you can have peaches. I really like peaches.
Yes means you can be a veterinarian.

Yes means you can dress up and be Arielle.
Yes means if you really want something, you can have it.

Yes!

Nyah Sky Eberhardt, age 6

I love YES! I hate NO!
Can I have 100 stuffed animals? Yes!
Can I have 100 pieces of candy? Yes!
A million bunny crackers? Yes!
Can I have ice cream for dinner? Yes!
Can Mommy play and play with me? Yes!
Can I have a house made of candy? Yes!!!
Can I dance around the whole house and have a concert?
Yes!
Can I have a collie dog? Yes!
Can I have puppies all around me? Yes!
I love yes! I hate no!

Yes to Avocados

Heather Rader

Yes to green meat scooped out with a spoon.
Yes to pits held by toothpicks balanced on a glass
waiting to sprout. Yes to "I'm gonna grow an
avocado plant, Mama, and plant it in the garden
by the string beans." Yes to skins of a black
that's green and a green that's black. Yes to
bumps. Yes to thumbprints that say, "I'm ready
for guacamole." Yes to firmness that says,
"Patience." Yes. Yes. Yes. Yes to slices and chunks
and mash. Yes to high-chair trays covered in green
smears and bibs with pocket surprises. Yes
to black beans and ceviche and Avocado Lime Pie.
Yes to bright orange stickers that say: RIPE.

Yes, You May Wear Pajamas to the Movies!

Melinda Gates

It's a moment you probably won't forget.

In a truthful, mind-altering moment of profound grace, you wake up and see clearly. In that moment, in your car, in the middle of traffic, in the midst of an argument with your son, you get it. You are doing to him exactly what you are scolding him for doing. You are resisting his resistance.

"But I don't want to do soccer. I'm *not* going to do it."

"Well, I think you should at least try. How can you know you don't like it if you've never tried?"

"I don't want to!"

"Well, you're going to soccer and that's that. You can't spend your whole life saying *no* to everything!"

That's when the full force of your hypocrisy hits you. In that moment you experience your own deeply ingrained resistance. The world shifts on its axis; your parenting can never be the same.

As you turn the car around and head toward home, you silently thank your son, yet again, for inviting you to face yourself.

Over the next few days, you are stunned to see how often you push against your child. The sheer quantity of *no's* shakes you up. You begin to question some of them. Does it really matter if you postpone bedtime this once? Why can't he take a bath later? Why does he have to clean his room today? Will it kill him (or you) if he doesn't finish his dinner?

You start to redefine "nonnegotiable." You recognize that you've been on autopilot, acting on unquestioned assumptions about what has to happen and why. You begin to actually *feel* the weight of all these unexamined *no's*; their impact knocks the wind out of you; you can't imagine the burden they place on your boy.

You start to look for more ways to say "yes" and are confronted with a surprising assortment of unexamined feelings and beliefs. Most of your habitual responses involve some fear of the future: if he doesn't do this/learn this now, his future life will be compromised. But what about his *now* life, you start to ask?

You consider all you know about living in a vibrational reality and how your nonphysical reality (thoughts and feelings) determines, attracts, and creates your physical experience. If this is true, then you have to wonder what is being created in any situation if the primary vibration is resistance, resentment, and powerlessness? At this point, you're pretty sure this is what your son has been experiencing, more often than you'd like to admit.

Sure, you want him to feel the thrill of accomplishment that accompanies learning new things, following through, and doing what he says he'll do. You recognize that sometimes life requires us to do things we'd rather not. But if he's consistently learning under duress, you start to question what is actually being taught. That "because I said so" is more important than how he feels, right now? Have you been actually teaching him to distrust his own feelings, you wonder?

You're not on autopilot anymore. You begin to see that life itself is a miraculous stream of Yes. You don't want to push against the current anymore.

You look at this intelligent, curious, and passionate little boy. What would it be like to trust him to his own adventure while helping him develop the essential skills to navigate life's flow? What if your first priority were getting him properly oriented in the river, helping him experience the difference between fighting the flow and allowing it to carry him? What better gift could you give than nurturing his own source of guidance of what's right and wrong *for himself*?

And what better gift could you give yourself? Propelled by this deepening awareness, trust, and acceptance, you surrender to the loving and intelligent flow of life. You notice that life at home feels more relaxed.

You're always on the lookout now for ways to say "yes." Yes, have dessert before dinner. Yes, we can buy this new computer game, because I know it sparks your joy and passion. Okay, let's postpone the trip to the store until after this television program. Sure, why don't we leave the Christmas tree up a few more days? Yes, you can wear those sandals, even though it's pretty cold outside. Of course we can wear pajamas to the movies!

When fear activates your resistance, you give it to the Presence (God/Divine Source/Universe) first to discover if there's a valid need or if you're just reacting from an old pattern. Sometimes you find your answer is still "no," but your vibration around it is completely different. It loses the fearful, reactive, *pushing* quality. And because there's nothing to push against, you're getting significantly less push-back from your son.

You notice that as you release fear and tension, you are creating a space where your child can actually move toward you. As you begin to trust him more, you notice he trusts you more. Because he knows that you honor his thoughts, feelings, and choices, he is more open to hearing what you have to suggest. You are hearing "yes" from him more often.

He's still clear that soccer is not for him, but you can now celebrate his clarity and the fact that he is in touch with what he wants. Gratefully, it doesn't take him long to reorient himself in the river. Without your resistance to push against, he naturally turns downstream. You know you have fulfilled your most important role as you watch your son—and yourself—navigate the river of life with greater confidence, joy, and ease.

Thirteen

Jennifer Milich

It is one hundred and five degrees today in Brooklyn, there is no
    school,
and we have caravanned to your favorite, to Brighton, to swim
it is your thirteenth birthday
your friends are old enough now to help me carry the bags heavy
    with food,
the Q train is on time, the seminal views of Coney Island snake into
    view as we round the track
parachute, Cyclone, aquarium

if you had been born to a different mother, this would be your year of
    ceremony
you would have been dressed in white, touched on the head by
    someone holy
you would have studied for years, an ancient book in your hands,
the enormity of universe placed before you to wrestle, memorize, sing
stories of ghosts and redemption, of travel and sacrifice would be
    yours now,
and there would be some change in you, defined, like a new name

if I had given you any religion, you would have had training,
weekly meetings with tired friends after school, you would read
    Latin, or Hebrew,
the rabbi's hand on your shoulder, your eyes skipping over familiar
    hieroglyphs
you would have studied the passage chosen specifically for you
for the day and the hour you were born, 12:59am on West 14th Street

our car service driver speeding us across the river,
feeling responsible for your safe passage, cursing the unexpected
    construction on 6th Avenue
saying he would pray for you
fear tasting like metal and acceleration in my throat
as I got out of the car and crossed over four lanes of 8th Avenue traffic
    in my nightgown,
your father amused and nervous behind me,
paying the cab fare and collecting your car seat, your new clothes

today, your friends and I take you to the beach, we make you a
    campsite of
folding chairs, blankets, your favorite fresh cheese
we sit cross-legged around you under a borrowed yellow umbrella
many of these boys I've held as babies, some of them I've
    sung to, picked up from school, and today
in the hazy kinetic air I see a flash of the men they will become
they are clocking the surroundings, stretching their new bodies out
    against the sand
they chatter, close ranks around you, and your brother finds a way
to light the candles in the heavy wind, the one and the three,
cartoon stripes to match the box from Juniors
the little flames balance and flicker and we tighten our ring of chairs,
and wait out the crowds, until the littered beach belongs only to us
and all of the boys want to stay until dark

I think of other 13-year-olds on their birthdays, the importance
    of suit,
the gathering of family, invitation, the moment where the boy,
    the baby is lost
and his mother is returned a man who resembles him
the weight of this number is more awkward than I'd anticipated
we are both unsure of its result, we are awkward today, but your
    freckled cheeks still seem like mine,
the way you tend to the cat, your always upward-searching eyes

when I was pregnant I was connected for the first time to ritual,
to the women in my neighborhood

I carried your new body against me down Court Street,
and I belonged, sliding sideways into motherhood I was welcomed
    and I wanted church and cake
I wanted women around me teaching me everything to feed and
    to sling and to settle
and now at thirteen I picture you, if we'd lived far from Brooklyn
calluses along your strong hands,
a circle of women who have loved us gathering, reciting to you a
    warning as we send you
into the forest, fashioning the finest clothes to protect you,
    the luckiest talismans of their own children,
outfitting you with tools and food, and tricks against bear, poison

but your journey here is one beneath Wonderwheel,
our familiar highway passing the space of the Twin Towers,
your taco truck, the foggy swing of the Verrazano
you haven't had a proper ceremony, there are no shiny envelopes filled
    with money,
no caterer, there isn't any dancing
but you have Brighton, and the fierce love of your mother, the sound
    of your neighbors
and their thoughts on the porch
your initiation is one of sand, subway, the haze of your smoke bombs
    on our corner
and the match is in your hand tonight, the colors deep and drunken
as your friends and brother stand around you
dirty and sweaty and a little bit older today, they
make their circle as I watch
there is no officiant, no gospel
but they are singing your favorite song, and yes
I pray, and I send you out
the same

My Marcela

Erinn Magee

While living in San Marcos, Nicaragua, a small village nestled in the coffee-growing highlands, we were often bombarded with visits from peddlers, beggars, and religious enthusiasts. From our front gate we could purchase toilet paper, fresh bread, live turtles and parrots, mangoes, pineapples, or simply donate our old newspapers to the noblest of causes: outhouse use. We negotiated daily with the lady who collected our leftovers to feed her pig, an ex-contra soldier crazed by the war who only wanted the occasional cigarette and called me Blondie, and groups of children begging for whatever we would give them.

In one particular flock of children, led by the short little bully Luisa, who would spit on you if you told her you had nothing for her today, was a wide-eyed little girl who hung back from the pack, unwilling to hurl insults when pleads of *por favor* were unheeded. Something drew me to her and I found myself whispering to her to come back later, without Luisa and the gang. Later, she returned alone, and left shy and grateful for my once-read newspapers, the gently worn T-shirts, and a container of leftovers for her supper.

Eventually Marcela was hired to tutor our housekeeper's nine-year-old child, Carlitos, who was in desperate need of help with his homework. We purchased a bicycle to aid in Marcela's transportation to and from this new part-time tutoring position. Naturally, after an afternoon of homework, supper was provided at the dining room table and sometimes lunch for tomorrow, as well. Soon, Marcela had a job seven days a week. She would bring her two-year-old niece with her on Saturdays and eat lunch and play in the patio while Carlitos learned how to ride Marcela's bike under his watchful tutor's eye.

I knew little of Marcela other than that she was ten, eleven, and then twelve years old and lived in the scary part of town near the cemetery, where no *gringa* would ever go. I knew only that her father had died when she was a child, decapitated when he stuck his head out of the train window, and that she lived with her mother and older siblings. She helped me shop in the market and, on one excursion, we bought her first bra.

Suddenly, it was time for me to go. Life was taking us away from Nicaragua and onward to Panama. It was decided that anything un-essential for our new lives in Panama would be given to Marcela. We loaded up a bici-taxi with our goodies: mattresses, pots and pans, a two-burner stove, towels and linens, and headed to the shacks near the cemetery. I gasped as we stopped at her house. Black plastic sta-pled to wooden scraps framed her walls. Embarrassed, Marcela hur-ried the bici-taxi driver to dump her gently used treasures in the mud, and soon I was whisked away, back to home, the landscape a blur through my sobs.

The next evening, while I was musing over a cold beer in my empty house, flying out the next morning for a country I had never visited, an ancient and haggard woman came to my door. Assuming she was a beggar, I wondered what was left to give away. Instead, she asked for me by name and I walked outside to greet her. In Spanish she thanked me for the years of support for her daughter, Marcela. She told me what a good girl Marcela was, to which I wholeheartedly agreed. She told me how much Marcela helped her at home. Know-ing I had no children of my own, she begged me to take Marcela. To shuttle her to Panama to live with me. To give Marcela a future she would never be able to provide. Now, twelve years later, I still wake up in the middle of the night gasping with regret that my answer was not YES.

Beth Levine

Kevin Pochocki

I can only remember a little bit about my home. My dad said it was in Florida. I used to have a mom until she fell asleep. We had a pool and a swing set. I remember other kids and food in the back-yard, but once Mom fell asleep, I can't remember too much about home after that. Dad and I got into the car because he had to look for work.

Dad told me he was a doctor, but he had lost his license. We had to leave Florida because nobody wanted us there anymore, and he wanted a better place for his little girl. We stayed with people Dad called friends; but most of them were strangers, and none of them were very nice. Dad always promised me that the next place we were going would be the last.

A lot of nights we stayed in the car. He would pile blankets on me and tell me to stay hidden. I remember once when I woke up, he was gone. I was scared, but when Dad came back he had some clothes and doughnuts for me.

One time I had an accident and Dad got so mad at me because the car smelled. He said that it lost value and I cost him a lot of money. I started to cry; I wished that my mom would wake up and come get me. Some days Dad was really nice, when he wasn't sleeping, but a lot of the time it seemed like he cared more about his friends than he did about me.

One day he told me we had to start using my Grandpa's last name. So instead of Beth Bagel, I was Beth Levine. He told me about the city that Grandpa lived in and said that we would visit him some-day. He said that the trees were so big and green there, they looked like broccoli! He said Grandpa's name was Red because he had red hair, like me.

I kept asking when we were going to visit Grandpa Red, but now Dad said Grandpa Red was mad at us, and Grandpa Red blamed me and Dad for making my mom fall asleep. I said that was silly 'cuz Mom was just tired, and maybe Grandpa Red wouldn't be angry when she woke up again. That is when Dad told me she wouldn't wake up ever again, and that we would never see her until we all died, but that we would probably never see her because God didn't exist. I hated Dad when he told me that.

Every new place we went, Dad would drive around looking for friends. He would sell them pieces of paper with his doctor name on it, 'cuz he used to be famous and they were worth a lot of money. Sometimes Dad would get jobs cleaning places, then he would find new paper; this made him happy. Once he got me an American Girl doll with the money he made from selling them! I named her Beth, like me; we looked alike. She would keep me company when Dad was working and when he was sleeping.

One day we were living in an apartment and Dad told me that I didn't have to go to school because he would teach me everything that I needed to know. So Beth and me would stay inside and play. Dad told me not to answer the door for anybody. But one day, the landlord came in with some lady. The lady started crying. The police came and started asking me questions. I told them I was okay and Dad would be back and explain everything. But they brought me to a special home called a Foster. They took away Beth 'cuz they said it wouldn't be fair to the other kids. Dad never came to get me.

They gave me new clothes and a bed of my own. We ate and played and I was going to go to school! I liked school; I got to help with chores and getting mats out for the little kids to take naps. They said I was a good helper. One day I was out on the playground and a man came up to me. It was my dad. He told me he wanted to take me to lunch, but the car he brought me to wasn't his, and some lady was driving it.

The lady was really nice to me. She said they were going to bring me back, but we had to go somewhere called Arizona first. Dad looked old and bony. The lady told me they were going to Arizona to get Dad help. One day the lady left us; when Dad woke up, he was mad, saying she stole something from him and that he was going to die if he didn't find it.

We got to Arizona without the lady and got a trailer that was our very own. Dad found a job fixing things. Miss Melanie was our neighbor. I would usually have dinner with her; she gave me stuffed animals and clothes to wear. I told her I wished she was my mom. Dad got mad at her one day for going through our trailer when he was sleeping. She told me that she did it for my own good.

Not too long after that, Dad fell asleep on the couch. I couldn't wake him up. I went over to Miss Melanie's trailer and told what happened. She went over to check on him. When she came back, she told me Dad had passed away.

Miss Melanie found my Grandpa on the computer. Soon, Grandpa Red came to get me. He was old and wore a funny hat on the back of his head. He was strong, and when he started hugging me I felt safe. He was crying and calling my name over and over again. "Oh honey," he said, "You don't know how long I have been looking for you!" Grandpa Red's clothes smelled nice, and so did he.

"I have your mommy's old room all ready for you to stay in, Beth." I didn't want him to let me go. Grandpa Red asked, "Do you want to come home and live with me, Beth?" That is when I started to cry.

"Yes, Grandpa Red," I said, "Yes!"

Taking Yes to the End

Linda Saylor

Yes is like an open book,
Just turn the pages, take a look.
Yes is where life turns on a dime.
Yes makes decisions.
Yes can change your mind.
Yes is a place where conscious dreams form.
Yes can lead through open doors.
Yes invites you in and offers more.
Yes is the answer some give when you ask.
Yes could be your very best friend.
Yes is when fear of the unknown rescinds.
Yes is where the journey begins.
Let yes take you to where it ends.

Part Eight

Sincerity

Sincerely

Cedar Burnett

It's hard to go cold-turkey on bitterness. Becoming a troll takes years of practice and careful grooming—one doesn't simply go to bed with a rainbows and unicorns outlook and wake up as Edgar Allen Poe. There are disappointments to log, idealism to be destroyed, and doe-eyed love to be shattered before one can take up the mantle of a hate-everything elitist.

I grew up in the right time and place—the sad-camp city of Seattle in the time of grunge. I was the portrait of a rain-and-gloom-bred teenager who had come of age in an era of divorce, AIDS, anorexia, and navel gazing. I smoked clove cigarettes; I drank coffee like it was water; I shamelessly quoted Camus.

Guarded, dark, and always ready with a reductive summation, I wore the requisite late-90s artsy uniform of black polyester old man pants and child-sized T-shirts. I had tattoos and listened to Nick Cave and Elliott Smith. And I went to The Evergreen State College—a school known for being equal parts hipster, hippie, and unabashed nerd.

To further my internship, I took a work-study job at the school's Photo Center—a cavelike fox-burrow of underground darkrooms and nascent digital studios linked by dimly lit, fluorescent hallways. We sat in the dark and made lists of things we hated. We reeked of developer and ate only bagels.

The Photo Center was where the art hipsters converged—the ones who actually made things, if by "things" you mean enormous black-and-white portraits of the photographer lying naked in a wheat field next to a toaster/gnome/roadkill/bust of Nixon. They were very deep, these people. But at least they produced something tangible—something with weight and thought and time spent huffing film chemicals.

During my second year at college, I signed up for a course called Fictional Sociology, as much for the name as anything else. This class was populated with an entirely different crowd—more of the garden-variety dilettante critic—a snarky, unimpressed subset now so pervasive they rule the online universe.

These kids hated everything. Everything. Religion, art, convention—sure—but also anything remotely popular, anything loved, any norm, any tradition or sincere expression of emotion. This group ripped every act of creation apart. They had a dismissive answer for it all.

With no holds barred, the class rapidly devolved into a game of shock value and general meanness, like a real time Salon.com comment board. They may have hero-worshipped Lenny Bruce, but they much more closely resembled Tosh.0.

When we broke into project groups, there was a team that called themselves the "Poop Group" who subjected the rest of the class to scat videos of comely women defecating into men's mouths. Members of the class, in response to a vagina-shaped promotional poster for a campus production of *The Vagina Monologues*, retaliated with a giant papier-mâché penis left on the grassy knoll.

Everything we read that entire quarter dripped with sarcasm and irony. Every class discussion was a one-upmanship of "Who can care the most about which they care the least?" Nothing was sacred, nothing special, nothing beloved. Death? Cancer? Pain? Anything was fair game.

I had entered the class as sarcastic and bitter as they come. But being around so many hollowed-out, veneered, ironic kids broke me. The immersion therapy of being confronted with an extrapolated version of myself flipped a switch in my brain. It was the nightmare version of *It's a Wonderful Life*, with me as Jimmy Stewart watching beauty torched at the hands of sarcasm—every time a hipster sighs, an angel gets crushed by a DeLorean.

As the class wrapped up, I vowed to change my ways. I embraced sincerity and popular culture and cheesy, happy, Disney love because I had seen firsthand what I would become if I didn't. My ghost of Christmas future had a Bettie Page haircut, a film degree, and booze-wracked holidays spent daubing Bingo sheets at VFW halls with other jaded Stepford wives.

Nervously, I dipped a toe into the sea of earnest joy and kept at it until it was second nature. Even while working in the music industry and sales and freelance writing, I worked to beat back the dark thread of bitter acidity that threatened me every step of the way. When I felt myself wanting to give up and join the overwhelming wave of trolls and meanness on the Internet, I detoxed with videos of baby pandas and the heartfelt pleas of nonprofit activists fighting to make the world a better place. I bought cookies from the Girl Scouts. I gave money to Habitat for Humanity. I planted trees and signed petitions, sang along to Taylor Swift, and sent my blissfully irony-free three-year-old to a Lutheran preschool.

Still, the wagon was there and I fell off it on occasion. I'm not all sunshine and roses. I still pack some irony in my original 80s Muppet lunchbox. But my awe and genuine interest in the world make me say yes to sincerity far more than it says no these days. My real insurance is being a mom. There's nothing like parenthood to strip you of any illusion of aloof coolness or jaded detachment. You have to stay in the here and now. You have to teach what's right from what's wrong. And you have to look for beauty and joy in the midst of backbreaking work and struggle.

Watching the Care Bears movie with my daughter a few weeks back, I burst into tears as the bears and their cousins chanted, "We care!" much to the amusement of my pixie-like child.

I remember the first time I saw that movie in the theater with my Dad's girlfriend du jour, who was scoring major points for our cinematic field trip. I also remember, and I swear on my life this is true, that I leapt up in that theater and yelled, "We care! We CARE!" at the top of my lungs, my little fists pumping the air as I declared my allegiance to what was right and moral and, in its own way, profound.

At 35, I still want to be that girl. I want to stand up and ally myself with love without the mental hashtag of a sarcastic aside. I want to be honest and brave and unmasked. I want to always say yes. Because the truth is, I care. I really, really care.

Grumpy

Brittany Tobiason

When I sit down to write something cool, I always set my frown to grumpy. I do this to be likable. Pollyanna annoys. We all do like to indulge in irritation. Everybody appreciates an excuse, bingeing on the gluttonous intimacy of rationed vices, gritty confessions, the comfort of bitter jokes. We yearn for purging. We appreciate a good excuse. My indulgence plus your indulgence equals our comfortable cool. The place of us is in the city, like in a song, on a fire escape, waiting for a train. The symbiotic night is a crocodile's mouth for exchanging seedy neon words. They clean its teeth, render it cartoony, noir, unreal. We don't take ourselves quite as seriously as a sleepy detective, a desperate heiress, or a black-and-white kabuki of brick and cobblestone and telephone wires. So they make it okay that we take ourselves as seriously as we do: somebodies about to really become somebodies figuring that, to rise out of the muck eventually, one first must be in muck. This never happens anywhere nice.

Because dreams aren't made of the stuff of Kansas. Dreams do not want something they're already taking for granted. Fresh air, a completely real horse, this breeze with its dandelion-seed wish are euphoric beyond aspiration. What better than a shiver of happiness? We don't need shoes for that, or a portion of all the spilling cornucopia of our precious excessive opulence: the rings we don't know what to do with, the ugly gold, like potatoes sprouting in the dark, again, except that those guilty replacements of things into temporary nooks *could* so effortlessly quicken the breath, anyway—could be a hard, sharp *ooo* that ripples little fishes out of the chest and rain upon the cheeks, the hot eyelids, the dryness soothing into a Yes.

A Yes that could carry you into ecstasy. A quiet Yes, a fierce Yes, a burst of joy Yes, a cry of victory Yes, a timid, squeak Yes, a rumbid-a-bumbida Yes, a Holy Horseshit Yes, a finally, finally, finally Yes, an It makes perfect sense Yes, an I'll marry you Yes, an I'll have second helpings, please, Yes, a thank you, thank you, oh thank you thank you Yes is all you need. Knowing this secret will change you beyond the ability to intentionally lay it on a little grumpy, for effect, a little deprived, a little resistant, a little worse-faring than most, a little less skilled at laying it on a little syrupy.

We should all stop requiring misery of each other and make a game of training out of the sinkhole. A game such as reveling, a game such as observing, a game such as grinning about the many sizes and nuanced kinds of even more genuine smiles as they happen. When I get up from my manufacture, leaving the shabby coat on the chair, I spin in rainbow sunbeams, dancing like a fool. I jump up and down pretending to hold a microphone. I can no longer be contained by sham dissatisfaction.

Lamborghini

Wayne Lee

So I'm in the waiting room at the chiropractor's and the receptionist from Puerto Rico has stepped out for a moment and her phone is ringing every five seconds *duh duh duh-duh-duh* in the same electric-piano-vibes timbre as the opening chords from Neal Hefti's jaunty theme from *The Odd Couple* and the woman next to me with wet tennis shoes is knitting a gray sweater for herself and when "Girl from Ipanema" comes on she nods that yes she has heard the song before and she keeps on knitting and answers no there won't be any other colors just gray and the receptionist comes back with fresh lipstick and I return to reading a year-old issue of *Car and Driver* that features an 887-horsepower Lamborghini that at $448,000 is a bit out of my price range although the driver's seat does look surprisingly comfortable.

Of Swans and Demons

Melanie McFarland

There's an expensive café in downtown Chicago that's less of a place to buy coffee than a temple to caffeine consumption at its most luxurious. I don't remember what it is called, forgive me; I visited a few years ago, and most of my memories from that time are lost in fog. What I can recall is rendered in blurred borders and irregular shading. I know I paid too much for lunch and ate too fast to savor the food's aesthetic value.

My most distinct memory is of a glossy coffee table book they were selling—published, of course, by the roaster that owned that café. This lovely, idiotic bauble featured shots of fashion world glitterati, each of them twisting in unnatural positions for the camera and sharing wisdom about the role that coffee plays in their fabulous lives. Among the featured subjects was a self-portrait by a photographer who famously struggles with bipolar disorder, and what sliced through the haze about his entry was part of his quote: along with exercise, he said, coffee helped him keep "the Gray Demon" at bay.

The Gray Demon. *Of course,* I thought. *That's what it's called. That's the Thing that's killing me.*

The people I come from have an interesting relationship with depression and tears. They are not unique in this; in a culture that has made the pursuit of happiness part of its doctrine, the weepy are tolerated at best. My family, however, has legacy with the sadness disease that spans generations. We've all inherited at least one version of depression, one item or more from a matching set of ancient, cursed weapons that attack its wielders and never parry.

But shush, never speak about it; for the love of Jesus, keep it secret! To name something is to give it substance and a skin, to acknowledge its power. It stands to reason, then, that not naming it wills it out of existence. Well, it's a theory.

Anyway, it explains my mother's and sister's reaction when at some point during my teens, sobs exploded out of my face for no apparent reason and with no obvious trigger. The tears flowed into the syrup on my pancakes after Sunday Mass. They materialized while we were all watching our favorite sitcom. In response, they would applaud with gusto.

"Acting!" they'd coo as they clapped, adding thunder to the squall that had interrupted everyone's good time. "Bravo!" My mother nicknamed these sudden fits of weeping "the dying swan routine," as if I were engaging in some elaborate form of improv, expecting a shower of roses. This was not a performance; truly, I had no idea what this thing was. An error in my soul's code? A virus? My mother assured me that my outbursts were entirely my creation, which meant I had the power to stop them ... and she really wished I would.

So I created a warding chant—a passionless string of *no-no-no-no-no-no-no* or *don't-don't-don't-don't* silently repeated when I felt tears tickling my insides. I trained my facial expression to retreat into blankness; my internal alto sang the sound of the universe as I knew it, *no-no-no-no-no-no, don't-don't-don't-don't*. This created a barrier, an interior dam behind which the sorrow pooled and sloshed.

Soon there was no more applause for the Dying Swan. Maybe the audience noticed the dying never ended; maybe they tired of the show. Yet the swan's invisible feathers outnumbered the dust motes we rearranged with rags and lemon oil every Saturday morning. They choked the air, muting our interactions. Surely my departure for college was a relief for all. I took everything with me, the swan's down, the stagnant water, and something I had yet to discover: a spiky ovum that washed up on a riverbank, waiting for the right conditions to germinate.

This is where it started, I think, these emotional collapses unrelated to skinned knees and bruised feelings. Eventually the ovum found purchase, growing into a beast in my belly, all incisors and claws and razor-sharp scales, circling and gnawing, circling and gnawing. It enjoyed a decades-long gestation, and it felt as if it would never pass out of my body.

I know now that the Gray Demon put it there. But for years, I refused to acknowledge its paternity, let alone its existence. *No-no-no-no-no-no, don't-don't-don't-don't.* Get rid of it. Bury it under avalanches of work and career plans. Move, start fresh. Surround oneself with friends, connect the ego to bylines and raises, to accolades, to pats on the back from the boss.

The Thing I Could Not Name loves ambition chained to unmoored confidence, lusts after those who build landmarks on fault lines. It wedged itself in our car's back seat each time my husband and I moved, first from Chicago to Portland, then to Seattle. It hid between cardboard boxes and trash bags full of crumpled clothes, waiting to be unpacked with the rest of the knickknacks, waiting for fissures to seep into.

To fend off the Demon's influence—which at that point, remember, was still just an error, a Thing—I reinforced the dam with artificial supports harvested from the type of false love and devotion that grow from letting strangers get too close too quickly. I threw huge parties in tiny apartments. Half-consumed mugs of wine slowly evaporated in glasses that lingered in my living room's corners, turning sour in the dark.

Not long after the Seattle move, my husband turned back to the south and re-relocated by himself, 300 miles away, to earn his doctorate degree. This sentence lasted six years. Which was fine! My workplace stock soared ever higher as I left old jobs for more prestigious positions, although most of my "pals" stopped returning my phone calls or pulled out of dates at the last minute, never to reschedule. Then the career started to sputter and I could see everything unweaving, all protections unraveling.

By the time my husband finished grad school, he returned home to a spouse collapsing into the gravitational pull of the black hole in her stomach, a portal carved out by the belly beast. He found me stalled at that hazardous junction of Not Wanting to Die and Not Being Up to the Task of Living. *I knew I shoulda taken that left turn at Albuquerque, part of me wanted to joke, but I couldn't remember the punchline, let alone much of anything else.*

It was around that time, days before a return visit to Chicago and the café epiphany, that I interviewed a famous news anchor for a story. At the end of our conversation, as I clicked off my recorder and thanked her, she did something uncharacteristic of celebrity subjects, and invited me to lunch. I responded with an action uncharacteristic of a person no longer fit for human company, and accepted.

There was a reason this woman was on the national stage. She had a gorgeous smile and a beautiful glow, and she did not waste much time with small talk over spring greens. Turns out she could see the Demon's mark on me. Some people who live through depression develop this power. This was not chastisement, but the act of an emissary from a peaceful nation, an ally who had sneaked into the war zone to reinforce the Resistance.

You have to acknowledge this, she told me. You have to admit that it's real, and navigate it. "And when you come out," she told me, "you will be new, tempered steel. Tougher and wiser. This is a forge. But you have to go through it." A forge, not a tomb. Who would have thought?

Then came the café, the discovery of the Demon's name, and soon I was ready to do the unthinkable—I drew it inside me. The Gray Demon and I spun and turned until I lost the ability to stand, until I was floating on boneless limbs; the beast within me swelled, howled, and gorged itself on deep, bloody bites of my innards. Together we twirled down, down, down into dark tunnels.

This was depression, at last. Good days felt like floating in a state of conscious hyper-sleep or some other name for stasis dreamed up by a science fiction author. Bad days were dry screams that lasted for hours and never summoned rescue.

God, how I loved it sometimes. The thought of being in the midst of large groups stole the air from my lungs, so I spent much more time by myself. It was the Best Lonely, one that didn't care what I wore, didn't judge as I poured grease down my throat. I grew a deep and lasting appreciation for my couch. Every day I looked at the sagging girl in the mirror and casually serenaded her with the simplest lyrics: *I hate you.*

She was the Dying Swan, handmaiden to the Gray Demon and, like him, it occurred to me that she was a poisonous illusion. It was time to fight my way out.

Here is where I must pause to say, some people never reemerge from the Gray Demon's tunnels. They spelunk naked in the blackness; they tumble into pits lurking around blind corners. Or, worse, some see a light and think they've found the way out at last, only to end up on a cliff ledge, staring into bright freezing sky. They jump anyway. Do not vilify those people or deliver the judgment that they took the easy way out. They got tired of being lost, that's all.

Many require medication to climb back to the world, but it only took a few conversations with friends to realize I didn't have the patience to discover which cocktail wouldn't leave me blank or suicidal. My doctor wrote me a prescription anyway. "We all need a little help sometimes," he said in the gentlest, most understanding tone, and I nodded as my inside voice silently said *no-no-no-no-no-no*. Anything but that.

And there was my answer. Literally, anything but that. Anything but no.

This is where the war really started.

I trained hard for the fight; I lifted weights and ran on the treadmill as a muscular man pushed me until every fiber that held my skin and bones together shuddered with fatigue. I made a list of things that made me happy once; I set about reconnecting with the very first item, dance, and the second, music. This time, random dance breaks would not be enough. The movement had to have strategy, it had to call down power from every pantheon. Fortunately I found a form that did called Nia, a blend of martial arts, dance, and healing movement that involved surrendering to the ground at the end. Very few people have heard of it—fine. More for me then. With every upward punch, sidekick, heel lead, and cha-cha-chat, I blasted away at shadows only I could see and hear. I cultivated genuine strength— not just in my body but my spirit, too.

Slowly I noticed my appetite for joy returning, growing, changing. My love affair for gloomy rock receded to the sound of ridiculously peppy pop music, and I delighted in belting out simplistic lyrics to the local college's music station as I drove down the highway, declaring to the world that this time, baby, I'd be bulletproof. I found profound meaning in chance occurrences: *"That hummingbird buzzed by right after I asked the universe if I should keep going." "The moon broke through the clouds tonight, just for me."* I skipped and strutted down sidewalks at ten in the morning, because a Sheena Easton song told me to, and just because.

I created Mel Rules, which include the following: "Dress to marvel." "Don't leave the house without at least two items of makeup on." "For every dark thought about someone who has abandoned, spend twice as long thinking about a loyal loved one." I started innocently flirting with random people, something I never did before. I didn't care how the energy was received, only that I radiated it.

This was my way of gathering great piles of red cartoon rockets with sparkling fuses, setting fire traps and dropping caltrops along well-traveled underground passages, of grasping my sword's hilt. I was ready. Then I noticed the beast wasn't devouring me anymore. For the first time in many years, I didn't feel it at all. Looking up from my battle plans, I saw the blazing truth that the darkness had dropped away.

All told, I wandered with the Gray Demon's labyrinth for nearly four years before I summoned the forces required to escape. That's a long time in the night lands. But there were unexpected discoveries down there, too, parts of my heart missing for so long that I forgot they existed. They were never lost; rather, they had been transformed by years of brining in salt and sorrow, softened into something fresh and tender, not weak. This new tenderness let me look at my world with new lenses. With this fresh vision, I see the many ways that pain begets pain in this world. That we can forgive while choosing to move forward in joy as opposed to returning to the places that hurt us out of habit, out of some idea of duty. I also see how many people, my family included, wear scars from their invisible demons. They all have names, but we are a vast company of sisters and brothers; we are legion.

I may slip and slide back through those tunnels at some point. The journey might be short or it might be another odyssey; the rapids may bounce me out of my raft into the underworld's rivers. Now I know I don't have to stay, I don't have to drown. Swans have wings for a reason.

The Vernal Equinox of Death and Kisses

Antonio Hopson

While the sun edged closer to the equator, waking the northern hemisphere while putting the southern half to sleep, and before the shadowy, blue-gray coldness of winter had thawed off the land, the vernal equinox of death and kisses lay crouched and waiting. It aimed to throw scented kisses through never-once-touched fields of dew-dripped grass.

But nothing moves without first being moved.

And so it was that every occurrence, every detail of the upcoming year—from the largest earth tremor or blighted storm to the smallest, splattered union of raindrop-to-river, of river-to-sea—had first been collected without first being conceived. It was a power spawned from actions gone past, actions that once existed and yet never could.

True.

There is a philosophy that suggests that the awesome power of a hurricane is first given birth by the most delicate flutters of a butterfly's wings.

No matter.

The vernal equinox of death and kisses would nevertheless arrive. Behind a shadowy veil of un-patterned patterns, it waited. Behind what is presented to our hearts, eyes, and ears and beneath the tingling of our skin, it slept, eternally patient, waiting for its time to come. And when it should come—dropping clues to earth disguised as events without cause—it threaded itself into reality like a grandmother's neatly stitched hem.

A teacher who had long lived the life of a spinster became giddy for no reason at all. It was fortunate that she did not bother to analyze or root out the reason for her good mood. Had she done so, surely she would have foregone her evening sorties into a nearby magical park. There, every evening, she watched a drowsy sun paint pictures on the horizon, where violet, pink, and red were used as purposefully as any artist's palette. The good mood was a nice change and was much preferable to the bothersome loneliness of loneliness. People saw her smiling for no reason at all. The subtle confidence it gave her attracted members of the opposite sex.

A young writer wondered romantically why the death of a grandmother had seemed perfect and timely. It was in the month of December, and she passed with the slightest hint of a smile into death's embrace. He had lived long in fear of her death, due to a self-pitying belief that a life without her would forever taint his world.

The writer might have continued believing death to be such a simplistic thing—a hunger, soaking up life as the bee soaks up nectar—but a wind, sent to him by the vernal equinox of death and kisses, smoothed the sting away. This wind brought the smell of life to his nostrils. It whirled under his arms, lifting him higher and higher—so high that he could see the birth of yet another new world.

In schoolyards across the country, tough-skinned boys kissed other boys. They cornered their prey and let the screaming victims have a "big one" right on the lips. Teachers noted this, smiled vaguely, and thought it a better alternative to games of war. For fun, little girls hiding in bathroom stalls traded underwear. Their parents were befuddled when unrecognized pairs of Cinderella or Pocahontas panties showed up mysteriously in the wash.

Motorists during their hellish commute were observed waving in fellow commuters who missed the merging tail end of a freeway on-ramp. From coffee mugs, they sipped delightfully at flavored lattes while listening to Vivaldi's "Largo e Pianissimo Sempre."

The vernal equinox of death and kisses touched everyone in some fashion or another. It rapped gently at the doors of their lives like a forgetful stranger who does not know he is knocking at the door of his own home. If caught mired in that analyzing little mood that wishes like the wind to knock down every sign, every tree, and every blessed flower that braves a new day, the people failed to hear its desperate but quiet clues to be savored, cherished—Yes! even worshiped. To them, testimony of its existence would not be recognized until finally, it had gone—a ripened, sweet stench left in a star-crossed trail.

. . . and once again the world became gray.

Beneath their cooled world, perhaps while drinking tea, they might pout, saying: "I hardly remember spring at all." And then, in a sudden moment of realization—a moment that reveals the hauntingly sweet departure of time and space—they might turn back to their windows and wait, hoping to hear the footsteps of the not-so-familiar stranger who had entered their lives in such a stealth, and in such a hush, they could only be aware of his re-return after once again he is walking away.

What Yes Means to Me

Dan Phillips

Yes, I'm smart
but yes, I've done dumb things
Yes, I'm usually kind
but yes, I've been mean
Yes, I'm flawed
But yes, I've risen above my flaws
Yes, I'm loyal
and yes that doesn't waver
Yes, I know much
and yes, I can learn more
Yes, I've been up
and yes I've been down
Yes, I've hated
But yes I've forgiven
Much is covered by yes
Positive and negative

Part Nine

Shadows and the Call

The Subtlest Yes of All

Karen Fendig Hoffman

Subtlety is an art, and it can appear both in the question and the answer. There is the obvious, the yes of the eagerly accepted job offer, of "I do," of passionate kisses and clothes on the floor. But what of the questions asked and answered between the lines? It is in these spaces that life's profundity and largesse often hide, and they are sometimes best filled in with an almost imperceptible yes. I'm sure that sometimes I have been unwilling to acknowledge these questions or have not allowed myself the option of answering with an uncertain yes. I've battened down my hatches, been too full of myself, too arrogant or stubborn to consider another point of view, too angry and self-righteous. Too alone. I've said no. Who knows what I've missed? Sometimes subtle doesn't have a chance. It's as simple as being too primitive to appreciate anything but a landslide stopping just short of my feet. Providence provides. You can't finesse the boulders. Heavy lifting. This I know.

Twenty-six years ago my daughter, Lindsay, was born. She died when she was three. A letter of condolence arrived from a dear friend and in it she wrote of a love affair. I was momentarily confused. A love affair? Did she think I was having one? With whom? And then I understood. She was referring to my relationship with Lindsay. Love affair, indeed.

Lindsay was born on a day bursting with the sunshine and tulips of spring. Her birth was so easy I was as stunned by that as I was by her arrival. She was the first grandchild in my close-knit family, and I had several friends with babies born that year. There was much excitement to share. Every day offered a swirl of love, happiness, and joy. I could never have imagined my life feeling this beautifully intense. I could not get enough of this creature, this gift, my child. She was like the air I breathe and sometimes I had to take myself away from people, from busy-ness, from life, and just go sit with her alone, holding her in stillness and quiet. Then one day, turning on the dime of a phone call, life changed irrevocably.

The call came on the day Lindsay turned six months old, and it relayed the results of a CT scan that had been ordered because she was not developing age-appropriate head control. I hadn't been worried; there were lots of theories. But the films revealed a brain malformation. Brain malformation. The words do not sink in easily. I didn't worry much at that point. Lindsay seemed fine. She ate, she slept, she giggled. But in reality, there was plenty to worry about, and so it all came to pass, slowly, over time. It was not long before the moment came when I realized I could no longer hold the ordinary hopes and dreams that the everyday miracle of children engenders. It was not realistic. Instead, I found I was standing at the edge of a cliff, looking into a void, with a mind stunned into blank silence. It was actually not that uncomfortable. The old saw is true: I was too blissfully ignorant to be scared. I opened. Grace abounds in the un-likeliest moments.

Some of you reading this may know how stories like Lindsay's unfold, but for those of you who don't, I would say that the main thing is that there is no certainty in the life of a child like her. None. It's true that life is uncertain for all of us. We are, however, skilled at ignoring that truth. We treasure the illusion that we are in control and that we can say no to whatever we fear or don't want. But I couldn't. I could not say no to Lindsay. I could not ignore the truth or conjure even the most far-fetched illusion. There was no normal, no room for expectation, no taking of *anything* for granted. There was day after day of knowing absolutely nothing except what was happening in the moment. Uncertainty was bald-faced and relentless.

The next two and a half years could be described as one long appointment, one long stretch of time filled with unanswered questions, surprises, surgeries, seizures, hospital stays, things Lindsay couldn't do, and things she would probably never do. Over time Lindsay collected fourteen doctors, had nine surgeries, and had more hospital stays and diagnoses than I can remember. She never attended day-care or preschool, but she did attend intervention programs and had multiple weekly appointments with physical, occupational, and speech therapists. Still, she never sat, spoke, crawled, walked, held anything, or ate enough to thrive; she was fed by a pump through a feeding tube as she slept. She died one night shortly after her third birthday, in her sleep. This is what her life can look like on paper. None of it tells you anything that matters.

It could have been easy to focus on the negative, on the sharp edges of the facts above. And I cannot tell you how hard it was sometimes. I do not know how to describe the physical and emotional exhaustion, the strains on a marriage, the ups and downs, the dashed hopes, and the fear that could not help itself from creeping in, all revolving around your child, life's most precious and beloved gift. But as I said, grace abounds.

I have always been amazed by the amount of grace I have received in my life. I deserve no more than the next person. Maybe I look for it. I am so grateful I was open to it and was therefore able to accept with love and courage the gift of Lindsay. I did not do it alone. With grace and faith, and in all good company, I carried Lindsay into her uncertain future. By doing so, I achieved a reality for both of us that is a blur of beautiful memories and is a story of love and happiness, adaptability and resilience. Lindsay lived a very full, fun, and happy life. She loved Big Bird, swimming pools, and parties. She rode on ponies, sat in tire swings, and went down slides, just not the way you might imagine. She had the life every child deserves. There is too much to write of the beauty of her life. Trust me on this, or ask anyone who knew her. Still, even hearing all of that would not tell you anything that matters.

Our lives are stories and the in-between of all of this lies within them. This is one that tells you something that matters. Shortly before Lindsay turned three, I took her shopping to buy her a birthday dress. I settled on two dresses for her to choose between. In no uncertain terms, she found a way to let me know which dress she wanted me to buy. No big deal. No. Big deal. At first I thought that I might be imagining things, but several times I showed her the dresses individually and she responded in the same way each time. I came to understand that her distinct and consistent responses could only mean one thing. Choice A was a yes and Choice B was a no. It was a singular communicative event in her life, and for a child who cannot speak, point, or barely move, it was a miracle. Even so, it's not the miracle that matters. What does matter is that I was given the grace to appreciate it, to be present in that moment and be made aware of the grandeur of this tiny, almost imperceptible yes. To become a person for whom that was more than enough. I felt humbled to my core, slain with gratitude and love for the universe that had given me this gift. That is what matters. It's what mattered then, and it's what still matters now, some twenty-three years later.

Lindsay's first and only yes was her parting gift. It has become a part of me, as have the gifts of her lifetime. The hard-won knowledge that love can only be unconditional. That beauty, simplicity, and serenity are most easily grasped by living in the moment, and by living there with acceptance and gratitude. That timeworn assumptions can be adapted or discarded. That reality can create walls or opportunities and we get to choose. That we are never alone, and that fear is an ugly invention of our minds. These were gifts freely given, and I am here to pass them on.

Quietly, and in some unknown language, you may be asked a question to which you cannot imagine an answer. Do not be afraid. From somewhere you will hear or remember the word "faith." Grace will fall from the sky. Breathlessly, and on a moment's notice, you will say, with courage and gratitude, yes.

Yes to All Feelings

Noriko Oki

Thank you
I'm happy
Love you
I'm lucky

I'm embracing all the feelings
Even enjoying
Aches and pains

When sad and lonely
Sob and cry
Always feel better
To let go and surrender

Illustration by Noriko Oki

Oakland

Caitlin Enwright

Oakland, California, is ripe for tragedy. Sitting mostly on old marshland, it tempts a large earthquake to liquefy it, begging the San Francisco Bay to flood in and fill the cracks and holes its residents have been obsessively picking at for decades. I heard there was a large native population here before everything was ruined. They buried their dead close to the water and consumed large amounts of shellfish. The area is named Shellmound, except there's an Ikea on top of it now. Technically it's in Emeryville, but who really cares?

I moved here eight months ago amidst a deteriorating relationship and the dejection fifteen years in the soggy Emerald City had left me with. In my mind California had become the promised land. Doesn't it always? I imagined myself sun-kissed and barefoot, plucking juicy Meyer lemons from my tiled patio and eating nasturtium salads while doing yoga. Somehow I would have long blonde hair and sing folk music until I eventually just turned into Joni Mitchell praising the glories of California land. Somehow a new me would emerge into the sun, a me who was never able to bloom under the perpetual overcast sky of the Pacific Northwest. California I'm-a coming home!

According to the FBI, Oakland is the third most dangerous city in America, behind Detroit and Flint, Michigan. I moved here in July and reality hit me like a bag of oranges. I moved to a neighborhood in West Oakland named Ghosttown, sometimes referred to as the Dirty Thirties, rarely called Hoover-Foster. If you search Hoover-Foster, Google will correct you with the parameters of an area called Ghosttown. Wikipedia describes it as a place known for its violence and blight. One could write a whole book on accepting life here, but Novella Carpenter did that already. She lives two blocks away.

I was terrified at first. Afraid to walk from my front door to the car. Constantly checking over my shoulder on the way to the mailbox. The stench of shit baking in the sun from fifty feral cats hung in the air. I'd fall asleep to the lullaby of screeching neighbors and thudding furniture. I often wondered if what I'd just heard was a firecracker or a gunshot. I was rattled by the sensory assault. I was inundated by domestic violence, homelessness, drug use, prostitution, poverty, and trash. My feelings were helplessness and fear. I wanted to notice the small acts of kindness in my world and to see the hidden beauties. But Oakland doesn't work like that.

My first winter here brought the worst drought in history, which ended in early February with a couple of days of heavy rain and a homicide next door. My psyche felt tainted with death and chaos for days, until I finally realized there was a hidden beauty Oakland had to offer. A man giving up the ghost while our neighbors stare in part horror, part amazement. The quiet moments between sirens and arguments.

The communal sense that we're not just living but surviving. Oakland is like a mangy feral dog with distrust for humans. But if your adoration is persistent, it will reward you with its dark shining underbelly. To quote Joan Didion, "The apparent ease of California life is an illusion, and those who believe the illusion real live here in only the most temporary way." To live here with permanence, you must accept the unacceptable. You must say yes when you thought you would say no.

Oakland is a pulsating dot on the map of mysticism, throbbing like a migraine. When you say yes, and give in to it, the pain recedes, and what's left is the rhythm of humanity.

The Call of a Word

Shannon Perry

Yes is a verb crying for justice in the streets
lined with police in riot gear.

Yes is an adjective, the tangerine sunset
sparkling on the still river against darkened hills.

Yes is a noun, the voice of a small child
the wordless smiling face of a misunderstood pit bull.

Yes is the woman who lays down the yoke
of the job in the market, the endless cycle of laundry, dishes,

fear that he will come home won't come home.
Yes waits patiently without judgment.

Yes is power, the surge
of the tide, no backwater eddy clinging to swamp roots.

Yes is the bell ringing in the valley calling.
Calling us to our better selves.

Yes is the word calling us home.

Suit Up

Jill Cooper

In this one you are sitting in a tweed jacket with your broad back to the camera. Did we plan it that way? Or was it one of the candids? Your head is turned to the left, almost but not quite looking back over your shoulder. It is your profile. At 20, I think, my little brother—my baby brother—has become so handsome.

I notice through the lens on my square format camera you look like Matt Damon. I know everyone says that, but I see it now. You are turning one side of your face away from the lens to hide a pocket of pimples on one of your cheeks. These portraits are for your girlfriend so you are careful, still, like a big summer cat. You are saving your usual joking for later.

As your sister, I have never noticed your features in just this way before—through the lens. I have not ever attended to the spirit in your brown, brown eyes the way I do today as your photographer. They are deep tunnels into your expression, caves under a strong shelf of earnest forehead.

Behind you now are the gnarls of roots from the base of an ivy-encased tree trunk. They will work perfectly in the image, I think, with the tweed, with the shape of your nose and the lines in your thick brown hair where the gel has been combed through and dried.

Later I will spend hours in the darkroom with this image, bathing the photo paper in attention, light, chemicals, and time. There are other pictures we make that day on the cliffs of San Clemente. The sky is a big laughing blue mouth above the heart of an abandoned mission, whose white stucco is succumbing to the knots of bougainvillea, palm, and wild lemon trees. With hammering heart, a hummingbird dives and sparkles, a flying jewel appearing and vanishing in a blink.

I am using a tripod to still the camera, to catch your motion as you leap up into the open window with its wide ledge for a prepossessing shot. A modern boy—okay, "a man," you remind me—in these beautiful ruins. You smile, and we talk about bicycles, my kids, pasta, the sky, treasure hunts, and angelfish.

I reload more black-and-white film while you tell me how you will have a picnic and surprise your girlfriend with your framed image. I listen. We scan the mission and landscape for more settings. Everywhere is perfect. And your crisp white shirt, rare tie, and wingtips make you look vintage from behind the lens. As if you are not of this time.

Now we wander to the dark, shaded place by this old tree. And you rest on something broken on the ground. Maybe it's part of an old stone bench used by some contemplative monk. And it's in this moment when you turn your head that I think how dear you are to me. I think how lucky I am to have this kind brother, who looks a little like Matt Damon, who so often makes me laugh, who is this day as somber and adult as the old tree.

I take the shot, and it's the last on the roll. We are out of film, so this is the last image I will make of you today, of your back and profile turning away. As if you are going away somewhere. A good ending to the series, I think. You give me one of those young man hugs with one arm and say thanks.

Later this evening, you will call and say, "I know I haven't told you this in a pretty long time, but I want you to know: I love you."

And I am happily pain-free at this moment. I pack my camera bag and plan to head to the darkroom—still free of knowing that this is also the last image I will ever make of you again. It's the last time I will ever see you in this short life of yours.

Now, decades later, I see you in the hills and tiny flowers, in the trees and bright sun. You are breathing through the clouds, laughing with the night crickets. You say, fold the words that describe your sadness into a gold origami of the heart. Fold the sting of grief inside you. Knead it deep into your love, where the alchemy of divine wholeness rises in the presence of that dark silence.

Every day is precious. Allow it all as it is, you say, a green leaf of grass twirling in your teeth. Every day, suit up.

Dawn and Mary

Brian Doyle

Early one morning several teachers and staffers at a grade school are in a meeting. The meeting goes for about five minutes when the teachers and the staffers hear a chilling sound in the hallway. *We heard pop pop pop,* said one of the staffers later.

Most of the teachers and the staffers dove under the table. That is the reasonable thing to do and that is what they were trained to do and that is what they did.

But two of the staffers *jumped,* or *leapt,* or *lunged* out of their chairs, and ran toward the bullets. Jumped or leapt or lunged—which word you use depends on which news account of that morning you read. But the words all point in the same direction—toward the bullets.

One of the staffers was the principal. Her name was Dawn. She had two daughters. Her husband had proposed to her five times before she said yes, and finally she said yes and they had been married for ten years. They had a cabin on a lake. She liked to get down on her knees to work with the littlest kids in her school.

The other staffer was named Mary. She had two daughters. She was a crazy football fan. She had been married for thirty years. They had a cabin on a lake. She loved to go to the theater. She was going to retire in one year. She liked to get down on her knees to work in her garden.

The principal told the teachers and the staffers to lock the door behind her and the other staffer, and the teachers and the staffers did that. Then Dawn and Mary ran out into the hall.

You and I have been in that hallway. You and I spent years in that hallway. It's friendly and echoing and when someone opens the doors at the end of the hallway a wind comes and flutters through all the kids' paintings and posters on the tile walls. Some of the tiles are clay self-portraits by kindergarten kids. Their sculptures were baked in a kiln and glued to the walls and every year there are more portraits, and pretty soon every tile on these walls will have a kid's face, and won't that be cool?

The two women jumped, or leapt, or lunged, toward the bullets. Every fiber in their bodies, bodies descended from millions of years of bodies leaping away from danger, must have wanted to dive under the table. That's what you are supposed to do. That's what you are trained to do. That's how you live another day. That's how you stay alive to paint with the littlest kids and work in the garden and hug your daughters and drive off laughing to your cabin on the lake.

But they leapt for the door, and the principal said *lock the door after us,* and they lunged right at the boy with the rifle.

The next time someone says the word *hero* to you, you say this: There once were two women. One was named Dawn and the other was named Mary. They both had two daughters. They both loved to kneel down to care for small holy beings. They leapt out of their chairs and they ran right *at* the boy with the rifle, and if we ever forget their names, if we ever forget the wind in that hallway, if we ever forget what they did, if we ever forget how there is something in us beyond sense and reason that snarls at death and runs roaring at it to defend children, if we ever forget that all children are our children, then we are fools who allowed memory to be murdered too, and what good are we then? *What good are we then?*

The Thing Is

Ellen Bass

to love life, to love it even
when you have no stomach for it
and everything you've held dear
crumbles like burnt paper in your hands,
your throat filled with the silt of it.
When grief sits with you, its tropical heat
thickening the air, heavy as water
more fit for gills than lungs;
when grief weights you like your own flesh
only more of it, an obesity of grief,
you think, *How can a body withstand this?*
Then you hold life like a face
between your palms, a plain face,
no charming smile, no violet eyes,
and you say, yes, I will take you
I will love you, again.

Dark

Fred LaMotte

I love blackness. O 3 a.m.! O womb, O voluptuous ink of poems, O Virgin of Montserrat, the blessed symmetry of zero, quantum vacuum gushing particles of night, oh fountain and fecundity of nothing, without your one eternal uncreated No this mad and multitudinous dance of yes could never be born: O Light is not enough, I love the Dark!

Contributors

Minna Aalto has a Master's Degree in Nordic literature and resides in Turku, a big enough small town on the southwest coast of Finland, and shares a precious everyday with her life partner, Michl Britsch. In addition to dancing, reading, and writing, Minna recharges her batteries in Yin Yoga, on walks, and through meaningful, deep-diving conversations with friends. She is also quite fond of heartfelt silliness. Minna started learning English at the age of 11, and English has become her soul language. In 2007, she founded Dakinia, a company focusing on delivering the message of Nia, a holistic movement form, giving courses on alternative takes on entrepreneurship and living, empowering women especially. Minna writes about her journey with Nia in her Finnish blog Nian matkassa, shares her poetry on www.wildwomanwashere.com, and composes and performs her own music as Minna Twice.

Liz Alexander, Ph.D., is a global hybrid: born in Scotland, raised in England, and a U.S. citizen since 2009. Her portfolio career can be summed up in one word: communicator. A former journalist and BBC TV presenter, Liz is the award-winning author of 14 globally published nonfiction books. She teaches strategic communications and storytelling for business impact. Liz also works with business leaders and teams in the U.S., U.K., and India through her consultancy, Leading Thought (www.leadingthought.us.com), guiding clients to communicate in ways that intrigue, influence, and positively impact their target market. Liz's constant companion is a black Labrador who thinks she's human, named Buffy (guess why?). They live in Austin, Texas.

Verity Arndt is a mother, wife, and spiritual counselor who is passionate about living this incredible life. After years of searching for real lasting joy and peace, and for insight into how the world works, she found what she was looking for. Since then, she feels absolute joy in showing others how to navigate life in a way that brings them the most joy and fulfillment. Her daily life includes home-schooling her three children, gardening, time in nature and meditation, raising golden retriever puppies, playing harp and piano, singing, and whatever else inspires her. More about Verity at www.verityarndt.com.

Ellen Bass, a poet and teacher, grew up in New Jersey. She earned an M.A. in creative writing from Boston University, where she studied with Anne Sexton. Bass's style is direct; she has noted, "I work to speak in a voice that is meaningful communication. Poetry is the most intimate of all writing. I want to speak from me to myself and then from me to you." Bass's collections of poetry include *Mules of Love* (2002), which won the Lambda Literary Award; *The Human Line* (2007), named a Notable Book by the San Francisco Chronicle; and *Like a Beggar* (2014). She helped edit the feminist poetry anthology *No More Masks! An Anthology of Poems by Women* (1973).

Bass has also written works of nonfiction, including, with Laura Davis, *The Courage to Heal: A Guide for Women Survivors of Child Sexual Abuse* (1988) and *Beginning to Heal: A First Book for Men and Women Who Were Sexually Abused as Children* (2003, revised edition 2008). With Kate Kaufman, she wrote *Free Your Mind: The Book for Gay, Lesbian, and Bisexual Youth—and Their Allies* (1996). Bass's honors and awards include a Pushcart Prize, a Pablo Neruda Prize, a Larry Levis Reading Prize, and a New Letters Literary Prize. She teaches in the M.F.A. program at Pacific University and lives in Santa Cruz, California.

Joanne S. Bodin received her doctorate from the University of New Mexico in Multi-cultural Teacher Education. She is an award-winning author, poet, and retired educator. Her book of poetry, *Piggybacked*, was a finalist in the New Mexico Book Awards. Her novel, *Walking Fish*, won the New Mexico Book Awards and the International Book Awards in gay/lesbian fiction, and placed finalist in three other categories. She is past vice president of the New Mexico State Poetry Society and has served on the board of Southwest Writers. She is currently on the board of the New Mexico Orchid Guild. Her poetry has appeared in *The Rag*, *La Llorona Poetry Anthology*, *Fixed and Free Poetry Anthology*, *Desert Sun Runner*, *Voices of New Mexico Too*, *JB Stillwater Magazine*, *NMSPS Albuquerque Chapter Poetry Anthology*, *Zingara Poetry Pics*, *New Mexico Mercury*,

200 New Mexico Poems Anthology, *The Storyteller's Anthology*, and *Adobe Walls 5*.

Hallie Bradley is a retired elementary school teacher and currently lives with her husband in Hood River, Oregon. She is working on a historical novel about the life of her mother, who kept a fascinating journal during the 1940s.

Cedar Burnett is a Seattle-based writer, mother, and professional rule-breaker. She once had lunch with Kenny Rogers and is unnaturally proud that Al Jazeera America paid her to go to Hempfest and write about it. Her work has also appeared in the *New York Times*, the *Washington Post*, *The Wall Street Journal*, Salon.com, *The Associated Press*, *USA Today*, MSNBC.com, Yahoo.com, *Huffington Post*, CBS.com, Fox News, *Fodor's*, *Alaska Airlines* magazine, and ABC-News.com, among other publications. She spent a summer in Boston wearing adult diapers for ulcerative colitis (then wrote a book about it). More at cedarburnett.com.

Rose Caiola could have easily been defined by her success in real estate, but she ventured far beyond the boundaries of the business world. She is a teacher, speaker, and expert practitioner of a number of disciplines that promote wellness—derived from ancient wisdom as well as cutting-edge science. Rose has studied neuroscience, Reiki, Tibetan Buddhism, Chinese herbal medicine, and various styles of yoga and meditation. She has received extensive training in neurofeedback, kinesiology, hypnosis, and Holographic Memory Resolution. Her journey informs RewireMe.com—the online community she founded for people seeking ways to learn, grow, heal, and transform.

Daniel Cammarn was born in Reidsville, Georgia, in 1987 to a military family that traveled around the world from the time he was born until 2002, when his father retired and settled down in Wakeman, Ohio. Since graduating high school in 2005, Daniel has traveled to two different countries and lived in four different states. He currently resides in Olympia, Washington, while attending South Puget Sound Community College.

Lois Colton retired from her work as a writing instructor at the Oregon State Penitentiary and moved to Hood River, Oregon, to be close to her children and grandchildren. She currently teaches ESL part-time to adult students at the community college and leads writing workshops for local writing enthusiasts. She chooses to live a life filled with energy and artistry—gifts bequeathed to her by her family. No family is perfect, but she knows the gifts of love she's been given. She never wants to stop being a learner and says "Yes" to way too many things.

Jill Cooper is a writer, poet, editor, and founder of Exult Road, the publisher of this book. Her writing has appeared in the literary and online magazines *The Raven Chronicles*, *The Floating Bridge Review*, and RewireMe.com. Jill has served as the director of a Buddhist publishing house and as a consultant to dozens of publishers across the nation. She offers all her creative endeavors as celebrations of life. She lives with her husband, Todd Murray, near the Columbia River in the eastern foothills of the Cascade Mountains of Washington state. Read her poetry and learn more at www.ExultRoad.com.

Jude Dippold was raised in a small Pennsylvania town on the western slope of the Allegheny Mountains. As a child, he spent countless hours in the forests surrounding his community, acquiring a lifelong love of nature that helps inform his writing and photography today. After graduating from Saint Vincent College with a degree in philosophy, he attempted to open a philosophy shoppe, but recession forced him to embark on a career in journalism and corporate communications. He is now writing poetry, pursuing his love of photography, and cycling his way into retirement.

Brian Doyle (born in New York in 1956) is the editor of *Portland Magazine* at the University of Portland, in Oregon. He is the author of thirteen books, among them the novels *Mink River* (big) and *Cat's Foot* (little; a friend of his says it is a "novella," but that sounds like a disease or a sandwich spread), the story collection *Bin Laden's Bald Spot*, the nonfiction books *The Grail* and *The Wet Engine*, and many books of essays and poems. His Huge Whopping Headlong Sea Novel *The PLOVER* was published in April 2014 by St. Martin's Press/ Thomas Dunne Books, bless their mad hearts. Brian James Patrick Doyle of New Yawk is cheerfully NOT the great Canadian novelist Brian Doyle, nor the astrophysicist Brian Doyle, nor the former Yankee baseball player Brian Doyle, nor even the terrific actor Brian Doyle-Murray. He is, let's say, the ambling shambling Oregon writer Brian Doyle, and happy to be so.

Nyah Sky and **Leela Rain Eberhardt** are sisters who live in Canton, Georgia. Nyah is 6. She loves animals, camping, and being silly—the grosser the better. She hopes to be a vet one day. Leela is 4 years old. She loves swimming, soccer, and chasing boys on the playground. She hopes to be a family medical doctor when she grows up. She loves to be just as silly and gross as Nyah. Both girls can most often be found making fancy art projects, giggling upside down, building campfires with Daddy in the woods, or riding on Marley, their golden retriever. These poems are the first of many published works, as they are both enthusiastic and creative writers.

Barbara Scott Emmett has published plays, poetry, short stories, erotica, and novels. *Drowning: Four Short Stories*; *The Land Beyond Goodbye*; and *Don't Look Down* are available as ebooks. Her latest book *DELIRIUM: The Rimbaud Delusion*, a metaphysical/literary novel was published in 2014 through Triskele Books. http://barbarascottemmett.blogspot.co.uk/

Caitlin Enwright is a 29-year-old human who lives in Oakland, California. She typed her submission to *The Yes Book* with a broken left hand and the cosmos painted on her cast.

Bash Evans is a 20-something California-born, Northwest-grown man of few words and many thoughts. He is a craftsman who admires detail and the beauty in quality. He is a student who yearns to become the master, and a master who yearns to learn. There are many things that may describe his life and the decisions he makes, but there is only so much he can tell you. You will more readily find Bash in his craft. You will find him in Down to the Root Studio. More at Downtotherootstudio.com.

Melinda Gates has dedicated her adult life to the exploration and relief of suffering, intuitively guided by a certainty that freedom, joy, peace, and immense power are natural birthrights of every person. As a Rosen Method Bodywork Practitioner and Divine Openings Guide, she offers counseling, coaching, and bodywork that invite others to remember the powerful magic of a yes-graced life. When not working, Melinda supports her un-schooled son in remaining true to himself through child-led learning and by facilitating his ability to live the life *he* desires. Learn more about Melinda's work and journey at www.AwakeningToYes.com.

Ille C. Gebeshuber, Ph.D., is an Austrian physics professor who has been living and working in tropical Malaysia since 2008. She works on developing new ways of doing engineering, inspired by living Nature's way. Ille's rainforest expedition teams are as diverse as the habitat they enter: veterinary medicine specialists, fine artists, engineers, biologists, physicists, economists—all together, learning, asking questions, listening to the answers, enjoying the beauty and togetherness, far remote from any phone reception or Internet connection, diving into a way of living that is different from our modern way, and yet can teach us much.

Martha K. Grant says YES to life through her poetry and visual arts in her Texas Hill Country studio, though she often must say NO to one muse in order to accommodate the other. She is now at work on a collaborative project, collaging her poetry into her art quilts.

Richard Grossinger was born and raised in New York City, attended Horace Mann School, Amherst College, and the University of Michigan, earning a B.A. in English at Amherst and a Ph.D. in anthropology at Michigan. With his wife (then girlfriend at Smith College), Lindy Hough, he founded the journal *Io* in 1964, then founded North Atlantic Books in 1974.

Between 1970 and 1972 he taught anthropology at the University of Maine, Portland-Gorham, now the University of Southern Maine, and between 1972 and 1977 he taught interdisciplinary studies (including alchemy, Melville, Classical Greek, Jungian psychology, and ethnoastronomy) at Goddard College in Plainfield, Vermont. Grossinger is the author of many books, including *Planet Medicine, The Night Sky, Embryogenesis, New Moon, Migraine Auras, On the Integration of Nature, The Bardo of Waking Life, and The Dark Pool of Light* 3-volume series.

Chris Grosso is an independent culturist, speaker, freelance writer, and musician. He created the popular hub for all things alternative, independent, and spiritual with TheIndieSpiritualist.com and continues the exploration with his bestselling debut book, *Indie Spiritualist: A No Bullshit Exploration of Spirituality* and his upcoming book, *Everything Mind*.

Jenn Grosso plays host to the dance of shadow and light, while smiling at the fleeting nature of it all. Embracing her inner sacred creative, she focuses most of her time on reading, writing, painting/mixed media, yoga, meditation, and picture taking. Connect with Jenn on her blog Perilsoftheliving.com, Facebook.com/perilsoftheliving, Instagram.com/jenn_grosso, and Twitter.com/Jenn_Grosso.

Chelan Harkin is a 25-year-old artist, healer, and poet, developing a deep trust that life is always leading her toward a deeper understanding of The Great Yes. Chelan is married to a wonderful man named Noah and they currently live in North Portland. She is also a hypnotherapist, and relishes her daily hemp-milk mochas. She loves to sing. Many of Chelan's poems come from this place of "YES!" so she is very happy that *The Yes Book* is creating a space where life-affirming voices can all sing together.

Karen Fendig Hoffman is a part-time barn hand and writer and a full-time wife and mother. She and her husband own a small coffee bar and live in Virginia. She believes in seizing the day, gently.

Lisa Hoffman-Reyes, Ph.D., is a studious fan of nineteenth-century epistolary exchanges, especially those penned by Robert Browning and Oscar Wilde. Her scholarly work focuses on Victorian aesthetic theory, gender theory, and mid- to late-Victorian poetry and prose. She teaches composition and literature at community colleges in Western Washington, where she always hopes for (and often secures) a classroom with a view of Mount Rainier.

Antonio Hopson is an author residing in Seattle. He is the winner of the Farmhouse Reader's Choice Award, Finalist "Best Short Story Anthology" EPPIE Award, Featured Writer at Hugo House and for NPR commentator Andrei Codrescu's journal, Exquisite Corpse. *Ogden Messiah* is his latest novel. www.Antoniohopson.com.

Lola Jones became an internationally known spiritual teacher when her book *Things Are Going Great in My Absence: How to Let Go and Let the Divine Do the Heavy Lifting* made its way to 135 countries by word of mouth. She created www.DivineOpenings.com, a virtual world where people take online courses, create community, enjoy or purchase her art, music, books, and audios. Many visit the site every day to see the inspirational short videos in the courses and the *Message of the Day*. Lola leads life-transforming Five-Day Silent Retreats in the U.S. and Germany, where results come with ease and grace, laughter and pleasure, instead of hard emotional work and processing. People are relieved to finally be able to stop the endless seeking.

Maureen Buchanan Jones is the Executive Director of Amherst Writers & Artists and leads creative writing workshops in Amherst, Massachusetts, under her business, Writing Full Tilt. Her poetry has appeared in *Woman in Natural Resources, 13th Moon, Peregrine, North Dakota Quarterly, Letters from Daughters to Fathers, WriterAdvice, Equinox, Calyx,* and *Chrysalis.* Her book of poems, blessed are the menial chores, is available on her website: www.writingfulltilt.com. Maureen's novel, *Maud & Addie,* is with Writer's House of New York. She holds a Ph.D. in English Literature.

Faith Keolker is a native of England. Faith came to live in Hood River, Oregon, in 2006, where she started a home care business with her husband. The beauty of the Columbia Gorge has reawakened Faith's creative voice, and she now writes poetry in her spare time. She is currently working on a collection of "traditional poems for our time" and is passionate about writing in a traditional, classical style.

Sally King is the author of the novel *Heirs and Graces* and the upcoming sequel *Folly in the Mist.* She is a mum and a businesswoman who owns 100k Hairdresser, a training company for hairdressers. She squeezes her novels and other writing in when she can, but acknowledges that it's all so much less effort since embracing author and teacher Lola Jones's motto to "just say yes."

Maria Kute is a reformed academic of the English variety (M.A., literature, University of South Florida) and an unapologetic perpetual student of music, creative writing, communication disorders, psychology, and the Internets at large. Born and raised in Louisville, Kentucky, she has taught piano and voice to many students in the Tampa Bay Area, and introductory writing and research courses to several college students of Clovis Community College, Eastern New Mexico University, and the University of South Florida. Within a few years, she hopes to finish her (re-) schooling and practice as a speech language pathologist, for she stands awestruck by the human ability to learn and utilize language in all its complexity, wonder, and abstraction. Currently, she is a resident of Las Vegas. When she hasn't been able to convince her husband to enjoy the glutton's paradise that Vegas offers, she watches her two dogs and cat goof off, makes giant pitchers of green and herbal teas, hikes, and studies for her communication disorders degree online with Utah State University.

Fred LaMotte is the author of *Wounded Bud: Poems for Meditation*, published by Saint Julian Press. He is an interfaith college chaplain and adjunct professor of world religions living in Olympia, Washington.

Dorianne Laux's most recent collections are *The Book of Men* (winner of the Paterson Prize) and *Facts About the Moon* (winner of the Oregon Book Award), both available from W. W. Norton. Laux is also author of *Awake, What We Carry*, finalist for the National Book Critic's Circle Award, and *Smoke*. She is co-author of *The Poet's Companion: A Guide to the Pleasures of Writing Poetry*. Widely anthologized, her work has appeared in many literary journals. She and her husband, poet Joseph Millar, are founding faculty at Pacific University's low-residency M.F.A .program. They live in Raleigh, North Carolina, where she teaches poetry and directs the M.F.A. program at North Carolina State University.

Alice Lee is the former editor and publisher of the Alaskan letterpress, Orca, and the former editor and publisher of Whistle Lake Press (Washington state). She received a Pushcart Prize for best of the small presses. Her poems have been published in many anthologies and magazines, including the *Alaska Quarterly*, the *Kansas Quarterly, Calyx, Crosscurrents*, the *New Mexico Poetry Review*, and *Adobe Walls*. Lee taught college English courses for more than thirty years and now enjoys her time gardening, writing, painting, and traveling.

Wayne Lee is a Canadian/American who lives in Hillsboro, Oregon. Lee's poems have appeared in *Tupelo Press, The New Guard, Sliver of Stone, Slipstream*, and other publications. His awards include the Mark Fischer Poetry Prize and the SICA Poems for Peace Award, and he has been nominated for a Pushcart Prize and three Best of the Net Awards. His third collection of poems, *The Underside of Light*, was published by Aldrich Press in 2013. Learn more: wayneleepoet.com.

Tara Lemieux is a mindful wanderer, spirited inspirationalist, and weaver of words. Although she may appear to be listening with great care, rest assured, she is most certainly lost in thought. She is an ardent explorer and lover of finding things previously undiscovered or at the very least mostly not-uncovered. To find Tara and read more of her musings, visit: www.mindfullymusing.com.

Erinn Magee is a Global Nomad currently living in Panama City, Panama. An educator, she is the high school principal at Balboa Academy. Her hobbies include teaching her dog Puchika Ines how to sea kayak, rocking in rocking chairs while reading great works of literature and student essays, and enjoying life in the company of her husband, Silvio.

Mariann Martland is discovering a voice in her life through words, poetry, art, inspiration, and healing. She is learning the difference between enforced silence in the despair of loneliness and chosen silence in the beauty of solitude; how silence can create both pain and peace. More of her writing can be found online at The Power of Silence www.thepowerofsilenceblog.com.

Dominique Mazeaud's calling for the last thirty-five years has been to answer "What Is the Spiritual in Art in Our Time?," a question she has lived as a gallerist, curator, artist, and writer, but mainly as a seeker preferring to call herself a heartist who does art for the Earth. She expresses her deep love for the Earth in ritual performances, community projects, and installations.

Patty McCabe-Remmell is a writer and editor based in Saint Petersburg, Florida. Since the 1980s she has written about topics ranging from gourmet cooking to auto racing and beyond, and is working on her first novel, tentatively titled *The Beautiful Year*. She also dabbles in poetry and essays on her blog, teaches professional writing at the University of South Florida, and fervently hopes the Rays do better this baseball season.

Melanie McFarland is a writer living in Seattle. Her work has appeared in *Variety*, Salon.com, the *Chicago Tribune*, *The Oregonian*, the *Seattle Times*, and the *Seattle Post-Intelligencer*. When she isn't writing, she is dancing and deepening her practice of Nia Technique as a Blue Belt instructor.

Kathy McGrath works as a consultant in Chicago. She has two wonderful, grown children, Andrew and Amanda, a husband, Ozzie—who also likes to write poetry—and her doggie companion, Buddi! Kathy loves writing and taking pictures of people and nature. She is part of the DivineOpenings.com community created by Lola Jones and is awake to a Grace-filled life, finding Joy and Bliss in the Presence.

Karen McSwain lives in a rural community that is equal distance between Seattle and Portland. She is an avid reader, an aspiring writer, and a lover of road trips and 1970s kitsch. Karen is a frequent contributor to *Yeah Write*, an online writing community for writers who blog and bloggers who write. She blogs at www.fatgirlboxing. blogspot.com.

Jennifer Milich is a poet and singer/songwriter who has been living and working in Brooklyn for the past 20 years. She studied poetry with Cornelius Eady at SUNY Stony Book and was the first student board member at Stony Brook's Poetry Center. She is also one of the founders of Scarlet Fox Letterpress, a creative collective that produces Salons based out of Ditmas Park; these events highlight and share the original work of artists in all mediums. The Scarlet Foxes just created and released Jennifer's first music video, "Calling Derek Jeter," viewable on YouTube.

Joseph Millar, poet, grew up in western Pennsylvania and was educated at Penn State and Johns Hopkins University, where he earned an M.A. in poetry writing. He worked as a commercial fisherman and telephone repairman for more than 20 years, and his accessible narrative poems, influenced by the work of poets Philip Levine and James Wright, often take working life as a means of engaging themes of class, family, and romantic love. In a 2009 interview for Pirene's Fountain with Charles Morrison, Millar stated, "We must have the ambition for our poems that they reach toward the sublime, that they speak from our own true selves and are grounded in the experience of our daily lives, including our dreams and hopes."

Millar is the author of several poetry collections, including *Blue Rust* (2011), *Fortune* (2007), and *Overtime* (2001), which was a finalist for the Oregon Book Award. He has received grants from the National Endowment for the Arts, the Montalvo Arts Center, and Oregon Literary Arts. His poetry has been featured on Garrison Keillor's National Public Radio program The Writer's Almanac and won a Pushcart Prize. Millar, who has taught at Pacific University, the University of Oregon, and Oregon State University, lives in Raleigh, North Carolina, with his wife, poet Dorianne Laux.

Michelle Motoyoshi has wanted to be a writer since she first learned how to scribble words on a page. Since then she has cobbled together a few accomplishments, like having her work performed with local theater groups, publishing three educational books for children, and writing articles for local and online publications. She has also managed to earn a Ph.D. from U.C. Berkeley. At present she heads up a small production company that has just completed its first short film, a mini-musical entitled "Practical Uses for a Time Machine." She plans to develop the film into a series. You can find out more about Michelle and her projects at www.facebook.com/PracticalUsesForaTimeMachine and at www.suddenwaffles.com.

Andrew B. Newberg, M.D., is Professor of Emergency Medicine and Radiology and Director of Research, Myrna Brind Center of Integrative Medicine, Thomas Jefferson University and Hospital. He is co-author of the best-selling books *Why God Won't Go Away* and *How God Changes Your Brain*, as well as *Words Can Change Your Brain*. He has also published several academic books, including Principles of Neurotheology and The Metaphysical Mind. His work focuses on the relationship between the brain and religious, spiritual, and mystical experiences.

Noriko Oki was born in Tokyo. After graduating with a B.A. in English & American Literature from Gakushuin University, she moved to California in pursuit of Art and Design and graduated from Otis/Parsons (currently Otis College of Art and Design) in 1992 with a B.F.A. in Illustration. She has been involved in a broad range of creative fields, including film production, computer animation, graphic design, editorial illustration, and toy design. Since 2000, Noriko has been living in Japan and is now based in Tokyo, where she paints and enjoys being a mother. Noriko is currently challenging and experiencing a cure of breast cancer naturally by enjoying, appreciating, and loving life. Painting is her tool to express, and by it she wants to reach out to anyone around the world who appreciates her art to heal and grow.

Dr. Marissa Pei is an inspirational speaker, organizational psychologist, corporate consultant, TV commentator, author, and talk radio show host of "Take My Advice, I'm Not Using It: Get Balanced with Dr. Marissa," a popular show on the Universal Broadcasting Network with over a quarter million downloads and 20,000+ regular listeners (www.ubnradio.com/drmarissa). She is the recipient of the 2012 Asian Entrepreneur of the Year Award, the

2007 Remarkable Woman of the Year, and the 2005 Role Model of the Year Award in Business and Media. Her book *Mommy, What Are Feelings?*, an interactive children's book illustrated by her daughters, has been recognized for helping autistic children all over the world. She has been featured as a television guest and commentator on major network shows including *Nostradamus: A Scientific Inquiry* (Discovery Channel), *Totally Out of Control People* (ABC/Discovery), *Busted on the Job* (FOX), *UFO's: Put to the Test and Monster Myths* (The Learning Channel); *Making It* (KTLA) and KUSI-TV News and CW6 in San Diego.

Doreen Perrine has published three novels through Bedazzled Ink, and her short stories have been published in anthologies and literary ezines including *The Copperfield Review, Lacuna, Freya's Bower, Raving Dove, Harrington Lesbian Literary Quarterly, Read These Lips, Sinister Wisdom*, and *Queer Collection*. Doreen's plays have been performed at Here Arts Center, WOW Café Theatre, Under St. Marks Theatre, and Manhattan Theatre Source in New York City. She is also an artist and art teacher who resides in the Hudson Valley of New York.

Shannon Perry is a generic Oregonian who has had the privilege of living in the Hood River Valley for 32 years. It has been a nurturing home for raising three daughters. The beauty of the valley inspires her every day and provides many opportunities to hike and explore. Shannon has written for as long as she can remember. She taught in the elementary grades for 28 years, and through that was able to nourish young writers. Now retired, she has time to explore her own writing. She lives with her partner, Stephen, and their cat, Bobcat, as well as Maxine, the box turtle she has had for 25 years.

Dan Phillips was born in Troy, New York, on August 30th, 1964. Raised mostly in California, he has been dabbling in poetry on and off since 1998, and lives in Santa Ana, California. He is single, and has had a lifelong interest in horror films and history.

Kevin Pochocki is a native of LaGrange, Illinois, who currently calls Littleton, Colorado, home. When asked about his motivation for writing, he explained: "I enjoy exploring the consequences of motivations, not so much the object, or fulfillment, of those motivations, but the collateral damage and the unseen impetus that is given to the actions of others. All of us are truly contingent beings whose lives are guided through the interactions we have each day. Whether our contact with others is by whim or choice, we affect the outcome of the lives around us." Kevin is a family man with a wife and two children. Outside of writing, Kevin enjoys cooking, gardening, and spending time with his children. "My job is to make sure that their lives are greater and the world benefits from having my children in it."

Heather Rader has always loved to write. Many times in her life, her journal has been her best friend. She's an educational coach, columnist, blogger, and author. You can find her at heatherrader.com to see what's on her mind.

Marleen Renders (*The Yes Book* cover illustrator) enjoys life and likes to say "YES!" as much as possible. She sees herself as a Homo Universalis, a woman of many talents. Marleen is gifted at letting the Divine do the heavy lifting and gives amazing Divine Openings sessions. Check out her blog at www.marleenrenders.com

Heather S. Friedman Rivera, R.N., J.D., Ph.D., is an author and past life researcher. She co-founded PLR Institute for advancing past life research. Dr. Heather speaks, writes, and hosts retreats. She is the author of *Healing the Present from the Past: The Personal Journey of a Past Life Researcher, Quiet Water,* and *Maiden Flight.* Learn more at www.plrinstitute.org, www.heatherrivera.com or email drheatherrivera@gmail.com.

Linda Saylor grew up on a farm in the Pacific Northwest. She has studied poetry, veterinary medicine, and animal husbandry, and is a master gardener with forty years of herbal and naturopathic experience. She and her husband moved to the interior of Alaska to build a home and raise two children. Linda uses a social network forum to share her daily diary, and that network of friends has grown into an audience of readers interested in off grid, rugged life.

Kay Schmerber is a retired middle school teacher and native Oregonian. Brooklyn, New York, was home for two decades, and she has been a partner to a gifted cherry farmer in Washington. She has one adult son and two adult stepsons. She lives in White Salmon and Portland, where she reads, watches movies, walks, and writes poetry. Two sisters, a 100-year-old father, and lasting friendships keep her honest.

Tosha Silver grew up thinking one day she would be a rabbi, a lawyer, or a weathergirl. But fate had other ideas. She graduated from Yale with a degree in English Literature, but along the way fell madly in love with metaphysics and yogic philosophy. For the last 30 years, she has taught many ways to align with the inner Divine. She lives near San Francisco and also writes a spiritual column at examiner.com. Her books are *Outrageous Openness* and *Make Me Your Own*. More information at www.toshasilver.com.

Kip Silverman is a writer of poetry, spoken word, bad haiku, and various other annoyances who lives in Portland, Oregon. Kip is a father of three incredible daughters and spends a good amount of time working to make this world a less horrible place through conversation and technology. He also is a great admirer of trees and a finely crafted cocktail and has at least once run for the office of the president of the United States. He currently has several strange Web sites, including http://politaiku.com/ and http://nirvanaflats.com. He is a member of the Portland-based writing group The Guttery. http://theguttery.com.

Silvio Sirias is the author of *Bernardo and the Virgin* (2005), *Meet Me Under the Ceiba* (2009), winner of the Chicano/Latino Literary Prize for Best Novel, and *The Saint of Santa Fe* (2013). A native of Los Angeles, he spent his adolescence in Nicaragua and currently lives in Panama with his wife, Erinn Magee. He also has a collection of essays titled *Love Made Visible: Reflections on Writing, Teaching, and Other Distractions*. The Routledge Companion to Latino/a Literature lists him among the handful of authors who are introducing Central American themes into the U.S. literary landscape.

Heather Sisson writes articles on teaching practices for Choice Literacy, instructional coaching for Lead Literacy, and is currently cultivating her inner poet while finishing her first novel. She enjoys reading and writing pieces with strong women who balance societal expectations with unabashed self-fulfillment needs. Heather lives with her husband, teenage daughter, and two black labs in Olympia, Washington, while her son serves in the U.S. Air Force.

Brittany Tobiason wakes up every day smiling. She plays house in various tents in a sunny valley in Western Washington state where she decorates her little snail shell of a golden trailer, grows rampant vegetables, writes in a hammock and feels like a little old man in spite of her pigtails in the rainbow sunset. She is a freelance writer and editor and can be reached at brittobiason@gmail.com.

Kathy Trapp has been creating stories and narratives her entire life. She has no memory of a time without books, spoken stories, or fantastical mental narratives to the everyday goings on of her life. The first story she ever wrote was an illustrated story of a lion and his friends that she wrote in kindergarten—a treasure she still has, thanks to her mother. It was because of the positive influence of her mother and her amazing elementary educators that Kathy became a lifelong learner. Today, Kathy is an early childhood educator and writes as a hobby.

Shirley "Rodeo" Landis VanScoyk is surprised to find herself a sixty-one-year-old widow and Nana living on a farm in Honey Brook, Pennsylvania. She cooks when she's depressed and when she's happy. She writes when she is something in between. She still has the world's crappiest kitchen.

Janet Ward has retired to White Salmon, Washington. She has two children and five grown grandchildren. Knowing that her children and grandchildren have grown up in a computer tech world, she has been writing her childhood memories of living during a time of back-porch iceboxes, wood cook stoves, ringer washing machines, and playing unafraid in the woods behind her house. She hopes that her memories of childhood will give the family a new perspective on "the way it was." She has visited all 50 states and numerous countries around the world. Her grandmother's sense of challenge and adventure contributed to the author's desire to step out.

Donna Wetterstrand is a modern-day enlightened spirit. She confesses to an ongoing, all-consuming addiction to evolving into the most expanded human she can be. Donna descends from a line of spiritual adepts, including two Mother Superiors and the Swedish mystic Emmanuel Swedenborg. Donna serves through her thriving life-counseling and business consultation practice. Most recently, Donna helped develop the well-respected Guide Certification Program currently offered through DivineOpenings.com. She is a mentor to the guides in training, and also offers sessions to anyone interested in learning how to manifest with ease and joy. Donna is also a published artist and writer and the mother of a wonderful daughter. You can contact her at djwetterstrand@gmail.com.

Linda Thompson Whidby is a freelance writer, poet, and essayist. She holds a Bachelor of Science degree in Secondary English Education from Kennesaw State University. Linda is currently writing her memoir and has been commissioned to co-author the memoir of American innovator T. David Petite. When she is away from her writing desk, Linda may be spotted indulging her love of interior design with a paintbrush, a sledgehammer, or a nailgun. She owns a home-remodeling business with her husband, Terry, in Marietta, Georgia. You can find Linda's articles, poetry, and essays at www.lindawhidby.com.

Genise R. White is a poet, writer, editor, and DJ. She has been writing poems and short stories since she was a young girl, and is soon to publish two books. She is also a Board Operator/DJ for two radio shows: Main Street Universe on Blog Talk Radio and her own creation, World Reggae Party, on Radio Fairfax, Fairfax, Virginia, where she reignites America with world reggae music. She volunteers for many community organizations and works as a substitute teacher in grades K–6 for the Fairfax County Public School System.

Brandi Leigh Whitehead works in the Los Angeles area music industry. She has been a promoter/manager for an underground hip-hop artist and worked as a lyric co-writer. She won the Indiana State championship for her short stories and poetry when she was ten years old, and has since published several poems. She is writing a book series for children and intends to create a record label that helps children in need.

Patricia Zylius is an incurable copyeditor. She gardens, practices tai chi, walks, and listens mostly to music written before 1750 and jazz. Her poems have appeared in *Caesura*, *Monterey Poetry Review*, *Sand Hill Review*, *Red Wheelbarrow*, *Catamaran Literary Reader*, *Ellipsis*, and *Women Artists Datebook*. In 2012 she published *Dear Sweeties: Tom Cuthbertson on His Dance with Cancer*, by her late ex-husband. Her chapbook *Once a Vibrant Field* was published in 2013 by Finishing Line Press.

Acknowledgments

This anthology would not have been possible without the talent, skill, and support of all those who cheered this project on and gave it life. I am more deeply grateful to the constellation of contributors and helpful friends and colleagues than any acknowledgment could possibly name. Writer Tara Lemieux is one of those to whom I owe a great deal of thanks. Her friendship and understanding of the project's deeper vision and her support and help on the Exult Road Web site all boosted my efforts.

I express gratitude, also, to my mother-in-law, Carol Murray. She may not have realized it, but her vital and consistent encouragement helped keep *The Yes Book* moving forward. I am thankful for the kindness, creativity, and acumen of artist and creative cohort Bash Evans and for the brilliance of editor Linda Carbone. Many thanks to Marleen Renders for the beautiful cover illustration and to Cheri Lasota for her book layout design work, advice, and care on this project. My spiritual mentor, author Lola Jones's contributions of initial inspiration, writing, and encouragement for the project infuse *The Yes Book* with creativity and pure, positive, life-affirming energy.

My son, Rome Esmaili, believed in this project from its first poem and prodded me to bring it to life. The smart edge he brought to the editing team polished several pieces to a bright shine. He is an exemplar of living a Yes life. I must offer thanks also to my eldest daughter, Anya Esmaili, who beams courage and was my first great Yes. And I want to honor my beloved mom and dad who raised me to lead an intentional, spiritual, loving life attuned to Divine Grace.

I offer a deep bow of thanks to the intelligent, savvy, funny, all-volunteer team of readers who helped in the difficult selection process. Oceans of gratitude to Jude Dippold, Heather Rader, Darlene Zidar, Saige Esmaili, Brittany Tobiason, and Lisa Hoffman-Reyes. Jude's strict adherence to quality helped keep the acceptance standards high. Heather's gentle affirming opinions helped me work with some of the writers to elicit their best writing during early editing stages. Darlene's deeply considered insights and reviews of various pieces served to help us focus upon depth and authenticity through the selection and editing process.

My daughter Saige's listening ear, keen eye, insights, and support were a gift to me and an enhancement to *The Yes Book*. My dear friend and spiritual sister, Brittany, served as a sounding board in early drafts of the book and editor of a number of contributions. Where there is editorial brilliance, Brittany's input is often in play. Lisa dedicated a great deal of her time as an editor and consultant. So much of what is excellent about this anthology is due to Lisa's cogent attention, genius, and love.

I would be remiss if I didn't thank all the contributors for their rousing enthusiasm for the project, as well as for their poignant writing. Their words will touch so many, and I celebrate each one of them and all their yeses! And, finally, I humbly offer a lifetime of thanks to my husband and best friend, Todd Murray, who loves life, *The Yes Book*, and me. I'm so glad I said yes!

Jill Cooper
Underwood, Washington
2014

A note from the publisher

EXULT ROAD

We thank you for reading *The Yes Book*! Exult Road is an indie press in Washington state and this is our first publication. Learn more at www.exultroad.com.

Review!

Reviewing is the number one way to thank the authors for their work and it helps others know more about the value of the book. Please share your thoughts on the *The Yes Book* with others. We invite you to write a review at Amazon.com or Goodreads or email us at info@exultroad.com.

Connect!

Please visit and "Like" *The Yes Book* on www.facebook.com/TheYesBookByExultRoad. Be sure to click the Notifications choice to see all weekly quotes and uplifting posts in your newsfeed.

Enjoy more!

Visit www.ExultRoad.com to view art and read more great literary, poetic, and inspirational writing on our blogs and "Featured Artist" pages. We also invite you to share your Yes writing or digital art and photography to be considered for feature on the Exult Road website. Write to publisher@exultroad.com.

CPSIA information can be obtained
at www.ICGtesting.com
Printed in the USA
FSOW01n1043171114
3496FS

9 780990 531708